Palgrave Studies in Marketing, Organizations and Society

Series Editor
David W. Stewart, College of Business Administration, Loyola
Marymount University, Los Angeles, USA

This book series will focus on the broader contributions of marketing to the firm and to society at large. It takes a focus more consistent with the original reasons the marketing discipline was founded, the creation of efficient systems through with societies provision themselves and match supply with the needs of a diverse market. First, it looks at the contribution of marketing to the firm, or more broadly, to the organization (recognizing that marketing plays a role in not-for-profit organizations, governments, and other organization, in addition to for-profit commercial businesses). Marketing plays a pivotal and unique role in the creation and management of intangible assets such as brands, customer lists and customer loyalty, trademarks, copyrights, patents, and specialized knowledge. Second, the series explores the broader contributions of marketing to the larger society of which it is a part. The societal effect of the modern firm, largely through the development of markets, can be seen in the per capita growth of GDP in Western Europe between 1350 and 1950. During this period, per capita GDP increased by almost 600%, while remaining virtually unchanged in China and India during the same. Marketing has played an important role in the improvement of the quality of life through increasing the number, nature and variety products and services, the improvement of the quality and convenience of these product and services, and by making these products and services more readily accessible to larger numbers of persons. The series will examine ways in which marketing has been employed in the service of social welfare—to promote healthy behaviors, family planning, environmentally friendly behavior, responsible behavior, and economic development.

Ross D. Petty

From Marking Products to Marketing Brands

A Legal Perspective on the History of Brand
Marketing

Ross D. Petty
Babson College
Wayland, MA, USA

ISSN 2661-8613 ISSN 2661-8621 (electronic)
Palgrave Studies in Marketing, Organizations and Society
ISBN 978-3-031-76777-7 ISBN 978-3-031-76778-4 (eBook)
https://doi.org/10.1007/978-3-031-76778-4

Cover illustration: © Alex Linch shutterstock.com

This Palgrave Macmillan imprint is published by the registered company Springer Nature Switzerland AG
The registered company address is: Gewerbestrasse 11, 6330 Cham, Switzerland

If disposing of this product, please recycle the paper.

This book is dedicated to my wife, Beverly A. Mcdonald, who has supported my various research and writing projects without complaint, asking little in return. She also has been my partner in love and life and the raising of our two wonderful children. I am blessed.

CONTENTS

About the Authors

Ross D. Petty is Emeritus Professor of Marketing Law at Babson College after being a faculty member for thirty-one years. He was a Faculty Research Scholar (2011–2019) holding both the Swirling Family Term Chair (2008–2011) and Roger A. Enrico Term Chair (1992–1997). While at Babson, Ross served on many committees including the undergraduate and graduate curriculum and twice on the tenure and appointments committee. He taught about 1600 undergraduates and nearly 4000 M.B.A. students. Ross is an award-winning reviewer who served on the editorial board of four academic journals, has published more than 100 articles, book chapters, and notes, and presented 115 times at various academic conferences and events. His work has been cited more than 1000 times according to ResearchGate. Ross is also the author of two books: *Branding Law: A Guide to Legal Issues in Brand Management* (2016) and *The Impact of Advertising Law on Business and Public Policy* (1992). Before joining academia, he practiced law with the U.S. Federal Trade Commission for nine years in various positions.

List of Figures

LIST OF TABLES

CHAPTER 1

Introduction: What Is Brand Marketing?

Abstract Harvard business historian Richard Tedlow (1990, 15) says that "[e]very great modern consumer product company achieved it success in part from owning established brands." The subject of this book is the historical evolution from barely noticeable product markings to the modern practice of marketing/promoting the brand itself. This book also uniquely examines the history of brand marketing from the legal perspective. Paul Duguid (2009, 3) notes: "The history of modern brands is to a significant degree dependent on the history of trademarks...." Other marketing historians such as Sivulka (1998) and Strasser (1989) all acknowledge that the evolution of trademark law contributed to the growth of modern brands. Thus, any history of brand marketing must necessarily discuss a history of branding law (Petty, 2016, 3–30). This chapter begins our discussion by introducing terms, concepts, and issues that are integral to the historical evolution of brand marketing.

Keywords Trademark protection systems · Brand promotion · Branding law · Branding products

© The Author(s), under exclusive license to Springer Nature
Switzerland AG 2024
R. D. Petty, *From Marking Products to Marketing Brands*, Palgrave
Studies in Marketing, Organizations and Society,
https://doi.org/10.1007/978-3-031-76778-4_1

Introduction

Today, brand marketing involves conspicuous brand identification and promotion of the brand itself. The history starts with branding animals and affixing brand markings on other sorts of products. Historically, such branding marks have been small and not very noticeable consistent with a lack of promotion of the mark. This book traces the evolution from mere brand <u>marking</u> to brand <u>marketing</u> where the brand identifiers are promoted to develop the brand's own image or personality that itself encourages sales of the branded product or service. Tedlow (1990, 14) calls brands "supernames" because they do more than just identify the product name, brands are promoted themselves to provide information about the product.

While some authors use the term "branding" without distinguishing brand marking/identification from promotion of the brand itself (e.g., Bastos & Levy, 2012), this book distinguishes identity branding from brand marketing to better illustrate the historical evolution from the first to the second. It should be noted that some of the history of brand marketing is often included and partially subsumed in the literature on the history of advertising since most advertising involves branded products and services (e.g., Laird, 1998; Lears, 1994; Pope, 1983; Richards, 2022; Sampson, 1874; Strasser, 1989; Tungate, 2013).

The modern concept of brand marketing (as opposed to branding) evolved from the concept of "trademark advertising" in the early 1900s. Stern (2006, 217) claims "brand" entered the marketing lexicon in 1922 as part of the compound "brand name" but Bastos and Levy (2012, 353) suggest that the term brand was in common usage at least by 1920. They provide an example of a quote from P. T. Cherington (1920, 150): "the appeal to the buy... by brand has become so general as to be in many lines of merchandise the characteristic rather than the exception method of sale."

Brand marketing may be particularly effective in situations where consumer evaluation of product attributes is difficult. Economists posit that some aspects of a product may be readily observed and evaluated by consumers before purchase. These are called search attributes. Product price, for example, is usually a search attribute. Other attributes may be readily evaluated upon use (experience attributes). Promoting the brand may be a useful short-cut for consumers, but one bad experience may cause consumers to eliminate the brand from future consideration.

Some attributes (credence) may not be readily evaluated by consumers at all such as long-term health benefits from taking a brand of multi-vitamin. Brand marketing may be particularly useful for products dominated by credence attributes because consumers won't experience negative aspects of such products to interrupt consumer attachment to the brand.

Product Functionality Promotion Compared to Brand Promotion

For decades, most modern marketing promotion has been recognized as a combination of promoting product (or service) attributes/performance/benefits and promoting a particular brand image/personality (Gardiner & Levy, 1955). Such promotions also may include price and purchase information. These elements tend to merge in most advertising. For example, identifying a retailer in a brand's advertising not only indicates where the product can be purchased but also might promote the retail brand. Similarly, providing price information also may promote either a value or luxury brand image.

Berthon et al. (2003) propose a more complex formulation of the brand versus product promotion issue. They offer the concept of a brand space that has two dimensions. The enacted-functional axis shows where brand promotion varies from promoting the meaning of the brand to promoting the functionality of the branded products. The second axis is the abstract-reified axis where at one extreme brand identity is more independent of the branded products in contrast to situations where the brand is closely identified with particular product(s).

They use these two dimensions to suggest four specific quadrants in brand space from the function-reified quadrant that is most closely tied to the product to the enacted-abstract quadrant where the brand is the least tied to particular products and their functionality and is the most abstract. Richard Branson's modern Virgin brand is an example of the latter. It started with music records and expanded to transportation, cell phone service, and other products and services even travel to outer space. It is promoted as a lifestyle brand that could be applied to almost any product or service.

However, these two dimensions are not independent of each other. Promoting product functionality over brand personality is likely to produce a brand that is closely identified with those products. Promoting the brand itself instead of product functionality may result in a brand like Virgin that is more independent of its stable of branded products. For historical exposition purposes, this book takes the more straightforward approach comparing the degree of brand promotion with the degree of product functionality promotion.

Although not all marketers aspire to have an all-encompassing lifestyle brand, the promotion and development of such brands are the highest level of brand marketing focused on the brand more than the product. While brand promotion can be factual in nature asserting low price or high quality, it is often done by image or emotional storytelling to create a brand "feeling" or personality about the brand that attracts consumers toward purchase. For example, in many fashion markets, consumers are attracted to the brand as much if not more than the design of the branded products. Recent data from Lippincott reveals that a strong brand drives even business purchase decisions more than price or product features. The study found that 39% of business purchases are driven by brand, versus 34% by features, and 27% by price (Lippincott, 2024).

This dichotomy between promoting the product's functionality and value versus promoting a brand image for the product parallels the historical debate between proponents of "reason why" advertising and image (or atmosphere) advertising. In the early 1900s, the former was considered "salesmanship in print." However, as the volume of advertising increased and many manufactured products became standardized with fewer unique features, it was increasingly difficult to attract consumer attention with factual advertising about product functioning.

Also in the early 1900s, the newly emerging science of psychology was applied to advertising. In 1912, an advertising proponent asserted was "possible through advertising to create mental attitudes toward anything and invest it with a value over and above its intrinsic worth." If consumers like a particular brand's personality (image) or feel an emotional connection to the brand, they may feel good about buying those branded products beyond liking their functionality and design. This brand promotion was often accomplished with symbolic images that would appeal to prospective consumers (Lears, 1983, 158–163).

Because of this dichotomy between promoting product functionality versus promoting the brand, classic trademark law does not protect functional aspects of product design. A product feature is considered functional if it is essential to the use or purpose of the product or if it affects the cost or quality of the product. If functional aspects of the product received trademark protection (that has no time limit), such features could not be used by competitors without a license thereby pre-empting patent law.

In contrast, protection of aesthetic aspects of product design or product packaging has evolved over time to now qualify for trademark protection if they are distinctive and indicative of the source of the product to consumers. This also may be called trade dress protection or protection against passing off and has a long legal history.

Again, consistent with this dichotomy the U.S. and other jurisdictions developed the concept of aesthetic functionality that prevents aesthetic aspects from trademark protection when those aspects are needed by competitors. For example, the color black in floral packaging and outboard motors doesn't affect product functionality but may still be helpful to competitors. Black packaging of flowers may be appropriate for Halloween, or funerals and a black boat motor may color-coordinate with boats of many different colors. Thus, although product color is typically considered to be part of the aesthetic design and potentially subject to trademark protection if it identifies the brand for consumers, courts have not protected product color in such cases where the color is functional (Petty, 2016, 890).

Exclusive Use and Protection Against Imitation

Today trademark law is so ubiquitous that it is often taken for granted. It is important to remember that protection against brand imitation is what allows consumers to search for the desired brand rather than analyze product attributes each time they shop for a particular good. If consumers can't distinguish between the original brand and its lower quality imitations, many are likely to stop buying the brand and will spend more time analyzing product attributes. Businesses then are less likely to invest in the brand and branded products generally if competitors can simply "free ride" on those investments (Posner & Landes, 1988). Therefore, exclusive use and restricting unauthorized imitation are essential for branding and a pre-condition for brand marketing to thrive.

Historically there have been four approaches to restricting imitation of brands. First self-regulation—the brand marketer decries imitation often informing customers how to distinguish imitations from the genuine article. Customers and merchants are then encouraged to purchase genuine articles.

Second, sellers may form private guilds that register members' marks and condemn imitations and imitators. Private guilds often gained legal authority over time leading to the third approach to restrict imitation—a governmental (or quasi-governmental) system to register marks in particular industries. In European countries these systems are established by the legislature or executive brand of government, initially at local government levels but more recently at the national (and even international) level. Finally, once the government is involved, it can authorize private lawsuits for injunctions and damages and even criminal prosecution of malicious and precise copying.

Dimensions of Trademark Protection Systems

When creating a system of trademark protection to enable brand marketing, there are several factors or dimensions that historically have been considered:

Requirements—what sort of marks or devices can be used as trademarks? Trademarks must be distinctive and identify the source of the goods. Made-up words or marks generally are acceptable, but generic or purely descriptive words are not. As noted above, packaging, and non-functional product configuration may also be eligible for trademark, trade dress, or passing off protection.

Establishment—to claim exclusive rights to a trademark, does the marketer merely need to use the mark on the good or must the marketer register the mark with a formal or informal authority? Or both?

Enforcement—is there any legal remedy against trademark imitation or are marketers limited to advising consumers about imitators and advising them on how to buy the genuine branded product? As noted above, legal sanctions could include damage awards, injunctions, and even criminal prosecution and penalties.

Goods Scope—can trademark infringement only occur with identical goods, similar goods, or related goods? This may depend on the intrinsic or acquired strength of the mark.

Strength and Similarity of other marks—how similar must imitative marks be to the original to be legally actionable? This may depend on the intrinsic or acquired strength of trademark, with stronger marks receiving broader protection.

Area of protection—is the mark only valid where it is used in commerce? Is it valid in countries where it is registered? Trademark treaties help expand trademark coverage to other countries.

Protection Goals—preventing consumer confusion about the source of the branded product is the traditional goal. Such confusion injures both misled consumers and brand marketers who lose sales to the imitative product. More recently, many countries consider prevention of dilution of a trademark's distinctiveness to be a legitimate protection goal even if consumers are not confused about the source of the product.

Competition and Trademark Monopolies?

Some marketers fear that restricting brand imitation too tightly can limit competition making it more difficult for marketers to offer and consumers to find similar brands and products. "Trademark monopolies" should be avoided if they limit consumer choice beyond avoiding deception (Lunney, 1999). As noted above, the legal system ultimately decides which brand identifiers are protectable under what circumstances.

For example, as discussed above, a broadly used modern brand name like Virgin could be protected in industries where it does not have any branded offerings. Similarly, a fabricated brand name with no pre-existing meaning such as Kodak may be given broad protection against imitation in other industries such as bicycles. However, a descriptive word like "apple" may be used by any seller of that type of fruit (as a product category not a brand) but could still be protected from other firms using Apple as a brand name for consumer electronics. Similarly, Virgin may be used descriptively for some products such as virgin wool or virgin olive oil.

CONCLUSION

Finally, it should be noted that the concepts of trademarks, branding or brand marking, and brand marketing are often intertwined if not confused. For example, the American Marketing Association endorses the International Trademark Association's definition of a trademark: "any word, name, symbol or device that identifies and distinguishes the source of the goods of one party from those of others." The AMA almost synonymously defines a brand as "a name, term, design, symbol or any other feature that identifies one seller's goods or service as distinct from those of other sellers." This book uses the term "brand identifier" for any name, symbol, etc. that is used to identify particular brands and uses the term "trademark" when discussing legal issues of trademark law. As noted above, this book also carefully distinguishes between brand marking or branding (discussed in the earlier chapters) and the development of brand marketing through the promotion of the brand.

References

Bastos, W., & Levy, S. J. (2012). A History of the Concept of Branding: Practice and Theory. *Journal of Historical Research in Marketing, 14*(3), 347–368.

Berthon, P., Holbrook, M. B., & Hulbert, J. M. (2003). Understanding and Managing the Brand Space. *MIT Sloan Management Review, 44*(2), 49–54.

Cherington, P. T. (1920). *The Elements of Marketing.* The Macmillan Co.

Duguid, P. (2009). French Connections: The International Propagation of Trademarks in the Nineteenth Century. *Enterprise & Society, 10*(1), 3–37.

Gardner, B. B., & Levy, S. J. (1955). The Product and the Brand. *Harvard Business Review, 33*(2), 33–39.

Laird, P. W. (1998). *Advertising Progress: American Business and the Rise of Consumer Marketing.* The Johns Hopkins University Press.

Lears, T. J. (1983). The Rise of American Advertising. *The Wilson Quarterly, 5*(5), 156–167.

Lears, T. J. (1994). *Fables of Abundance: A Cultural HIstory of Advertising in America.* BasicBooks.

Lippincott. (2024). *B2B Brands in the Human Era.* https://www.lippincott. com/insight/b2b-brands-in-the-human-era/#:~:text=A%20strong%20brand% 20makes%20B2B,well%20as%20how%20it%20communicates

Lunney, G. S., Jr. (1999). Trademark Monopolies. *Emory Law Journal, 48*(2), 367–487.

Petty, R. D. (2016). *Branding Law: Guide to the Legal Issues in Brand Management.* West Academic.

Pope, D. (1983). *The Making of Modern Advertising.* Basic Books.

Posner, R. A., & Landes, W. M. (1988). The Economics of Trademark Law. *Trademark Reporter, 78*(3), 267–306.

Richards, J. I. (2022). *A History of Advertising: The First 300,000 Years.* Bowman & Littlefield.

Sampson, H. (1874). *A History of Advertising from the Earliest Times.* Chatto & Windus.

Sivulka, J. (1998). *Soap, Sex, and Cigarettes: A Cultural History of Advertising* (2nd ed.). Wadsworth Publishing Co.

Stern, B. B. (2006). What Does Brand Mean? Historical-Analysis Method and Construct Definition. *Journal of the Academy of Marketing Science, 23*(2), 216–223.

Strasser, S. (1989). *Satisfaction Guaranteed: The Making of the American Mass Market*. Pantheon Books.

Tedlow, R. S. (1990). *New and Improved: The Story of Mass Marketing in America*. Basic Books.

Tungate, M. (2013). *Adland: A Global History of Advertising*. Kogan Page.

CHAPTER 2

Ancient Product Marking: Signs of the Times

Abstract In ancient times small marks were commonly used on goods. Some of these marks were maker's marks by the artisan or workshop that produced the goods. Others were merchant marks identifying the seller or shipper. While such marks identify the source of the products, over time some appeared to function as a promise of a certain level of quality or method of production. However, when medieval guilds took over the regulation of the use of such marks, they generally required marks be registered with the appropriate guilds and that individual artisans not promote their own marks. Only guild marks could be promoted for the quality of goods they represented.

Keywords Branding · Commercial signs · Artisan guilds · Merchant guilds · Commercial sign law · Commercial tribunals

INTRODUCTION

The practice of branding goods with small marks dates back to ancient times and has served several purposes over the years including indication of ownership, product origin or quality, and the ability to track goods in storage or transport (e.g., Moore & Reid, 2008, 421; Richardson, 2008;

© The Author(s), under exclusive license to Springer Nature   11
Switzerland AG 2024
R. D. Petty, *From Marking Products to Marketing Brands*, Palgrave
Studies in Marketing, Organizations and Society,
https://doi.org/10.1007/978-3-031-76778-4_2

Wengrow, 2010, 20). Often the brand or marking was simply the name or location of the person offering the product for sale.

Wengrow (2010, 22–23) posits that in ancient/medieval times, unbranded goods with no quality grading were sold in bazaar markets. Purchasers relied upon their personal relationship with the retailer to avoid being deceived about product quality and value. In contrast, brand markets in those days dealt in goods that were identified by brand, standardized (and readily substituted for one another), and strictly graded. Customers relied on the brand to be assurance of quality, but they had to watch out for counterfeits. Brand markets were generally wider ranging than bazaar markets.

Richards (2022, 9–14) searched cave paintings and ancient implements (e.g., marked ostrich eggs cups) for signs of ancient advertising, but the surviving evidence is inconclusive. For example, cave paintings of buffalo show apparent markings that might be branding or just natural markings on the fur—perhaps injuries. Potters' marks from 5000 to 4000 BC in the Near East could have been brands indicating the owner of the pots (like cattle branding) including their content. These marks also might be simple magical and lucky signs. Marking to indicate ownership is an important function of ancient branding and Richards (2022) suggests eventually such potter's marks evolved into promotional messages.

One interesting example from his history-of-advertising perspective was an Egyptian artifact from 3000 BC—a piece of wood that resembles a modern wine label or hand tag. The hieroglyphic inscription translates into the "finest oil of Tjehenu." This appears to be at least a promotional message, e.g., advertising, but could be an attempt to develop a brand even though the phrase is not sufficiently distinctive under modern practice to qualify for trademark protection (Richards, 2022, 14).

Proto-Brands?

Wengrow (2008) argues that using symbols for branding or marking goods occurred in the fifth and fourth centuries BC in Mesopotamia using seals and standardized packaging. In China from about the tenth century forward, the sale of goods differentiated by brand, by names of producers, sellers, product attributes, or other symbols became commonplace (Eckhardt & Bengtsson, 2010; Hamilton & Lai, 1989). This long history of product branding leaves the fundamental question largely

unanswered—were such brands and symbols used for mere source identification or actively promoted to attract consumer interest?

Moore and Reid (2008) examine what they call proto-brand artifacts
from ancient times. They cover several locations during the Bronze and
Iron Ages in the Indus Valley (2250–2000 BC), Shang China (2000–
1500 BC), Cyprus (1500–1000 BC), Tyre (1000–500 BC), and Greece
(825–336 BC). They conclude that proto-brands in all of these places
provided information about product origin and quality.

For example, the Indus Valley artifacts were small square seals (tiles)
that often contained an animal image that also may have provided a
brand-type image for the goods. Purchasers presumably would recognize proto-brand identity markings, but there is no evidence of whether
these markings themselves were promoted beyond identifying a particular
source such as the producer's name or location.

In contrast, the Shang China artifacts were clan crests representing
villages settled by specific families. The images on the crests were util-
itarian describing the products from that area rather than adding a
distinctive brand image unrelated to the product. Similarly, copper from
Cyprus was reputed to be high quality and so promoting the geographic
origin helped sell finished products made with Cyprus copper. The
Phoenician City of Tyre became well known for its distinctive, purple-
dyed garments and gray and red jugs decorated with red, maroon, and
black painted bands. These two products were sufficiently distinctive
themselves so that no additional brand identifiers were used.

Lastly, in Ancient Greece, competition among pottery makers led
to varied methods of differentiating one maker's wares from another
including some degree of brand promotion. Like Tyre, some makers
offered unique designs. They often would sign their products and include
a description of themselves or their circumstances. The seller's name is a
very basic form of brand identification and foreshadows the future use
of company owners' names and images (e.g., pictures of lions' heads,
bees, etc. as brand identifiers and to a lesser degree, as brand promotion
(Rogers, 1910, 30).

Other Grecian potters used images of power and prosperity. A cup
from Rhodes even promised that those who drank from it would be
smitten by Aphrodite (Moore & Reid, 2008, 428). As with other
locations, these images and messages appeared on the product or its
packaging.

By the second century, ancient trade routes that encircled the Mediterranean Sea and included most of Europe were being traveled under the auspices of the Roman Empire. Products marked with Roman names and symbols are found throughout this region (Drescher, 1992, 310). During the Roman Republic, marks were often brief—perhaps just the date. By the time of the Empire, the maker's name, the location and perhaps owner of the factory, and often a picture or figure were marked onto all sorts of products including building bricks, oil lamps, and metal instruments. Wine and cheese typically also included marks indicating geographic origin (Rogers, 1910, 28).

CASE STUDY: WHITE RABBIT SEWING NEEDLES IN CHINA

Fig. 2.1   White Rabbit advertisement from Richards (2022, 36)

The White Rabbit brand of Chinese sewing needles were sold during the Song Dynasty (960–1276) by the Liu family in Jinan. By this time, the Chinese government required the producers' names to be stamped upon the product which is the top line of the advertisement/wrapping label illustrated above. The family had a stone figure of a white rabbit outside their front door and the ad urged consumers to find the shop by looking for the rabbit. The ad also proclaimed, the needles were made of excellent steel and were easy to use. The firm offered discounts for dealers. This handbill was printed from a copper plate (Fig. 2.1).

The pictorial illustration shows a white rabbit either holding a needle or perhaps using a mortar and pestle to grind one. The image was designed to identify the brand for women, the likely purchasers of sewing needles, who were mostly illiterate. The white rabbit was considered good luck and associated with feminine energy based on a well-known legend. Thus, the symbol itself had added value to women potential purchasers.

While the ad contains product quality claims and provides a method for locating the store, the white rabbit illustration (consistent with the seller's name) appears to function as a brand identifier. The rabbit symbol also functions as brand marketing since the symbol itself attracts purchasers who feel an emotional attachment to the brand. Furthermore, the brand symbol itself is promoted to potential consumers, e.g., look for the white rabbit. It is considered the oldest surviving example of a marketing brand and is on display at the Museum of Chinese History (Eckhardt & Bengtsson, 2010, 215; Richards, 2022, 36).

CRAFTSMEN AND MERCHANTS AND GUILDS, OH MY!

In medieval Europe, guilds associations of artisans or merchants became a common form of production and marketing for a variety of products including pots, textiles, cutlery, books, metal works, etc. Guilds were generally formed by location and profession/output such as Sheffield Cutlery. Craftsmen guilds were formed to regulate entry into various artisan professions and to set and enforce high-quality standards for products there created. Often such artisan guilds were authorized by city or town laws to conduct quality inspections to remove counterfeits and defective products from the market (Cartwright, 2018).

Those artisans who agree to follow guild protocols for quality control and who pass inspection were allowed to use the guild's collective mark. Richardson (2008) argues that town/guild names functioned as collective brand identifiers, like today's collective trademarks, in medieval Europe and provided consumers with reputational information about the quality of goods (Duguild, 2012).

For example, in the fourteenth century Milan, Venice, Padua, Verona, Florence, and Flanders, the city seal was used to certify sealed woolen cloth had been made in the city in accordance with guild regulations. All drapers in each of those locations produced the same brand under a collective mark. The same was true for British towns producing textiles by the sixteenth century.

In the seventeenth century, France developed a national system for textile control where local guilds performed the first quality inspection. Those who passed qualified for a lead seal applied to the cloths. A second check was performed at the time of sale, often with government assistance. This system allowed for these public marks to be augmented with the use of private master's marks that identified the producer.

However, not all goods were subject to guild certification. For example, Venice imposed guild regulations on gold and silver smiths but not on glass makers. Maitte (2009, 12–14) suggests that Venetian glass products were unique rather than standardized. Variation was derived both from materials used and secret methods for processing them. Therefore, there was no standardized production method and no method of product quality inspection to support guild regulation for Venetian glass makers.

The second type of guild was the merchant guild. The merchant members of these guilds were involved in long-distance commerce and local wholesale trade. Many also were retail sellers of commodities both in their home cities and distant venues where they possessed rights to set up shop. The largest and most influential merchant guilds participated in international commerce, politics, and the establishment of colonies in foreign cities.

Merchant guilds enforced contracts among members and between members and outsiders. Guilds policed members' behavior because medieval commerce operated according to the community responsibility system. If a merchant from a particular town failed to fulfill his part of a bargain or pay his debts, all members of his guild could be held liable. When they were in a foreign port, their goods could be seized and sold to alleviate the bad debt. They would then return to their hometown, where they would seek compensation from the original defaulter. Merchant marks were used to identify the property of guild members during shipment and storage (Cartwright, 2018).

GUILDS AND THE LAW OF COMMERCIAL SIGNS

Not surprisingly, the widespread use of artisan and merchant marks led to demand for their formal legal regulation. The earliest example of a law that required merchants and artisans to brand their products occurred in

1266 England. Parliament required bakers to be licensed by a guild and to affix a mark or seal to each loaf of bread they sold. If guild standards regarding weight and price of loaves were not followed, the baker could be identified and held responsible by being pilloried or banned from being a baker for life. This law was enforced by local guilds throughout England. From 1300 to 1600, similar rules and formal laws were established to govern all sorts of crafts.

Schechter describes these artisan marks as liability marks because their purpose is to prevent low-quality products such as bread in the example above. Furthermore, guilds generally prohibited members from promoting their marks to gain advantage over other guild members (1925, 40–57). So, while guilds promoted their own mark as a source indicator for quality goods, individual craftsmen were prohibited from developing their own brands.

This system of guild control of commercial marks included both mandatory and de facto registration of craftsman marks. Some statute required these marks to be registered with the appropriate guilds. Other guild systems did not explicitly require registration but the guilds kept records of merchant marks in use so they could effectively police their use along with the use of the guild marks.

The second way that the law of commercial marks developed is through the resolution of mark disputes over who could use particular marks or their close imitations. During the Industrial Revolution, merchants overtook guilds in terms of political influence. Merchant marks became recognized as assets of customer goodwill so their unauthorized use or imitation should be restricted to prevent unfair competition. Such unfair imitation was recognized to potentially deceive customers and cause the loss of business to legitimate mark users (Drescher, 1992, 329–330).

Over time, reports of various tribunals and institutions that ruled upon such disputes formed a body of law that was then summarized by the legal scholars of the day. Because of these reports, we know this began happening in the 1300s (Fredona & Lopez, 2024, 5):

> … we can clearly discern an intensifying scholarly interest in the 14th century in the types of signs used in commerce, the marks hammered into the blades of swords, watermarks on fine paper, the symbols painted on merchant bales, the signs hung by hoteliers above their doors, and so on. Already by the 14th century and systematically in the 15th century, lawyers explicitly understood and discussed these signs as differentiating

indications of reputation and quality in need of protection. In all likelihood, this understanding was not new, but represented long continuities in the practice of local and long-distance trade going back to antiquity.

One important source of medieval commercial law was the Civil Rota a specialized merchant court established in the Italian City of Genoa. Established in the early 1500 s, by 1530 it was a leading tribunal for deciding commercial law disputes. For example, in Decisio CCI the court found in favor of an animal skins merchant whose products were branded: "these signs, commonly called marks, make a presumption that a thing belongs to the those whose little signs they are, because a marked thing is known by its mark" (Fredona & Lopez, 2024).

Decisions of this court and similar tribunals were collected, published, and widely distributed and followed. This is why decisions in other courts used language like the above when adjudicating disputes over identically marked goods.

Legal scholars during this time were able to review these reported decisions and present their analysis of legal concepts. They considered marks as more than just "badges of origin" but also as signs of reputation with potential commercial value. This commercial value was derived from the ability of marks to distinguish goods from different sources (Fredona & Lopez, 2024, 16).

In addition to ruling on cases of mark imitation, these tribunals also applied ancient property law to marks by deciding that a previously unused mark would belong to the first one who used it. They also developed rules for assigning mark ownership after a craftsman died or a partnership dissolved (Fredona & Lopez, 2024, 24–28).

European legal treatises of the time were limited to the continent. *Southern v. How* (1618) is generally recognized as the first English court case to examine the fraudulent counterfeiting of a merchant's mark—in that case to sell counterfeit jewels. Schechter (1925, 8–10) asserts the actual discussion in that decision was a judge's recollection of an earlier decision involving the sale of cloth using a counterfeit mark. Stolte (1997) argues this earlier decision was *Sandforth's Case* decided in 1584.

Stolte (1997, 509) states that this court decision demonstrates that Britain judicially recognized a common law right against trademark infringement at that time. Common law courts generally decided disputes by looking at past court decisions and legal principles rather than wait for statutes to be adopted. However, court decisions during that time were rendered in Latin and not widely reported which explains why *Southern v. How* is generally credited as the first English common law case to condemn trademark infringement.

References

Cartwright, M. (2018, November 14). Medieval Guilds. *World History Encyclopedia*. https://www.worldhistory.org/Medieval_Guilds/

Drescher, T. D. (1992, May–June). The Transformation and Evolution of Trademarks–From Signals to Symbols to Myth. *The Trademark Reporter, 82*, 301–340.

Duguild, P. (2012). A Case of Prejudice? The Uncertain Development of Collective and Certification Marks. *Business History Review, 86*(2), 311–333.

Eckhardt, G. M., & Bengtsson, A. (2010). A Brief History of Branding in China. *Journal of Macromarketing, 30*(3), 210–221.

Fredona, R. T., & Lopez, T. d. S. (2024). Commercial Marks and Sign in European Jurisprudence (1300–1600). In R. G. Bone & L. Bently (Eds.), *Research Handbook on the History of Trademark Law* (pp. 127–160). Edward Elgar.

Hamilton, G. G., & Lai, C. (1989). Consumerism Without Capitalism: Consumption and Brand Names in Late Imperial China. In H. J. Rutz & B. S. Orlove (Eds.), *The Social Economy of Consumption* (pp. 253–279). University Press.

Maitte, C. (2009). Labels, Brands, and Market Integration in the Modern Era. *Business and Economic History On-Line, 7*, 1–16. https://thebhc.org/sites/default/files/maitte.pdf.

Moore, K., & Reid, S. (2008). The Birth of Brand: 4000 Years of Branding. *Business History, 50*(4), 419–432.

Richards, J. I. (2022). *A History of Advertising: The First 300,000 Years*. Bowman & Littlefield.

Richardson, G. (2008). Brand Names Before the Industrial Revolution. *National Bureau of Economic Research, #13930*. www.nber.org/papers/w13930. Accessed 18 October 2012.

Rogers, E. S. (1910). Some Historical Matter Concerning Trade-Marks. *Michigan Law Review., 9*(1), 29–43.

Schechter, F. I. (1925). *The Historical Foundation of the Law Relating to Trade-Marks*. Columbia University Press.

Stolte, K. M. (1997). How early did Anglo-American Trademark Law Begin? An Answer to Schechter's Conundrum," *Fordham Intellectual Property, Media and Entertainment Law Journal, 8*(2), 505–547.

Wengrow, D. (2008). Prehistories of Commodity Branding. *Current Anthropology, 49*(1), 7–34.

Wengrow, D. (2010). Introduction: Commodity Branding in Archaeological and Anthropological Perspectives. In D. Brevan & D. Wengrow (Eds.), *Cultures of Commodity Branding*, (1st ed., pp. 11–34). Routledge.

CHAPTER 3

From the Decline of Guilds Through the Eighteenth Century

Abstract As the use of guild marks declined, the use of masters' marks became more popular and were supported by commercial tribunals. Furthermore, merchants often sought some sort of royal charter or endorsement to help distinguish their goods from others. However law courts were reluctant in supporting such commercial marks and in the case of proprietary medicines, often used poor quality as justification.

Keywords Guilds · Wedgewood · Royal Charters · Challenging Imitations

Decline of Guilds

As noted in the previous chapter, in many jurisdictions commercial tribunals were ruling that masters' marks were the property of craftsmen who first used them and they could transfer the marks to others by sale, rent, or inheritance (Belfante, 2017, 1130–1131; Maite, 2009, 10; Robertson, 1869, 414). This "ownership" of marks favored artisans over guilds as the latter began to decline. As countries became industrialized, guilds became outmoded—the craft industries were losing political

© The Author(s), under exclusive license to Springer Nature Switzerland AG 2024
R. D. Petty, *From Marking Products to Marketing Brands*, Palgrave Studies in Marketing, Organizations and Society, https://doi.org/10.1007/978-3-031-76778-4_3

and commercial prestige to merchant-entrepreneurs often selling factory-produced goods. Consumers became less interested in guild quality control and more willing to judge quality themselves with help from merchants of new product variations. The marketplace became a mixture of marks belonging to guilds, artisans, merchants, and master craftsmen. Artisan and craftsmen marks were becoming master's marks that could become signifiers of quality even without guild marks.

While such marks initially were not promoted to users to become assets of the mark owners, eventually some artisans sought to use and protect their own individual marks as the requirement of labels and certification were repealed. Sometimes such individual marks were similar in design to the guild mark used by the artisan before he sought to emphasize his own name and mark. Schechter (1925, 122) describes this shift from guild to masters' marks as changing from "liability" to "asset" marks or changing from quality control to starting to identify the origin of the product. This shift also set the stage for the development of a single law of commercial mark use rather than each industry with its own guild rules.

For example, drapers in Prato made wool fabrics for both the guild-regulated and unregulated markets. Similarly, cutlers in Thiers France used both a community brand on their blades and an individual brand for each master craftsman (Maitte, 2009, 4–5, 9–11). Many merchant entrepreneurs started as craftsmen who later became merchants. Domenico Bettini, a Bolognese merchant, started to produce silk veils. He registered his logo both with magistrates of Venice as a merchant and with the Silk Guild in Bologna as a silk producer (Belfante, 2017, 1135–1136).

ROYAL PRODUCTS

As noted in the last chapter, guild regulation became authorized and enforced by various levels of the government. As guild marks decreased in importance, some merchants sought to continue their products' association with authority by using nobility to promote and enhance their products' image. The earliest surviving record of royal approval of particular products comes from 1155, when Henry II granted the Weavers' Company a Royal Charter. By the fifteenth century the Lord Chamberlain formally appointed royal tradesmen with the Royal Warrant of Appointment. During Queen Victoria's reign more than 1000 Royal Warrants were granted. For example, some textiles were entitled to a royal brand such as the Royal Manufacture of Louviers. Such prestigious marks were probably more likely to be subject to unauthorized imitation because of their prestige (Maitte, 2009, 5). While the "Royal" label appears to be focused on the brand as much as the branded goods, it is not clear to what degree the "Royalty" of the brand was promoted independently from the quality of the goods.

Another method of obtaining not merely royal endorsement but also an exclusive monopoly on a particular trade was the patent. In England, the crown could issue letters patent to inventors who petitioned and were approved. The first documented letters patent to create a new industry in England was granted in 1331 to John Kempe and his company. Another early example of such letters patent was a grant by Henry VI in 1449 to John of Utynam, a Flemish man, for a twenty-year monopoly for his invention (Hulme, 1896). Some eighteenth-century trade cards promoted both a patent and royalty endorsements (Baird & Clifford, 2007, 156).

A third approach to connect to nobility was through the commercial use of heraldic symbols and signs (Mollerup, 2013, 17–23). Heraldry developed as a system of visual signs for the armor and identification of noble families (Barron, 1911; Fox-Davies, 1909). Perhaps it was inevitable that overlap would develop between these two systems. From medieval times, innkeepers would adopt the names and arms of local nobility. Other inns would adopt common heraldic images such as lions and boars. These uses of heraldry were seldom challenged. In addition, the King of Arms in England began offering arms to merchant guilds in the sixteenth century. This diminished the use of traditional rune-based merchant marks. For example, by 1725 Lady Christian Shaw of Bargarran used her family arms (pictured below left) on the package of the thread she and her daughters sold (Dawson, 2003, 115). Other marks, below right, combined elements of heraldry and runes (Rylands, 1910) (Fig. 3.1).

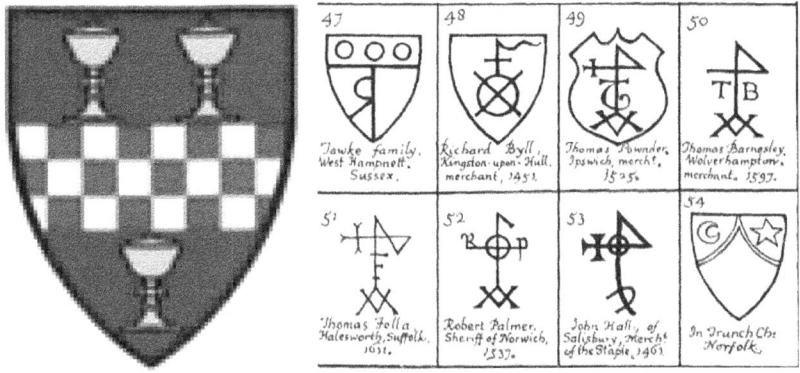

Fig. 3.1 Heraldry & Ruines from Dawson (2003, 115) and Rylands (1910, 38)

CHALLENGING UNAUTHORIZED IMITATIONS

While there are no objections to Lady Shaw's use of her own family arms, other commercial users of coats of arms faced unauthorized imitation. In 1740, an Italian merchant named Meyer who used a particular coat of arms in English markets to package his textile goods, discovered that a rival firm was using the coat of arms for the same type of textile goods packaging. The case reporter described this as a case of "passing off" making this one of the earliest uses of this term.

Meyer consulted with two lawyers. One, a member of the Court of Chivalry, felt the Court would have jurisdiction because this involved a coat of arms. The other lawyer disagreed, arguing that the commercial use made this sign a mark rather than a coat of arms. However, this second lawyer believed a case for fraud could be brought in the Chancery Court seeking an injunction and recovery of the costs of bringing the action.

Two years later, the Chancery Court's jurisdiction over commercial fraud was tested in *Blanchard v. Hill* (1742)—a case involving the stamping of an image and two words on playing cards. The trademark claim was based in part on an old and no longer valid law that gave the plaintiff the exclusive right to use the words "Great Mogul" stamped on his cards. Lord Mansfield refused to issue an injunction which would appear to support the repealed law that had created an undesirable monopoly. Despite this outcome, later court decisions would sometimes recognize this as the beginning of judicial trademark enforcement since the decision suggested that absent the special monopoly circumstances, an injunction may have issued (Schechter, 1925, 136–138).

According to Lauriat (2024), trademark cases continued with *Robinson and Roberts v. Wheble* (1771) involving the plaintiffs who had recently purchased the rights to the "Lady's Magazine." The new owners replaced the original publisher (Wheble) who then published his own version of the magazine advertising to be the only true continuation of it. After running an advertising response claiming to have an affidavit from the original owner verifying the sale, the two new owners filed the lawsuit for trespass claiming injury to their property.

Lord Mansfield agreed, comparing this situation to a cloth seller facing a competitor who was using the same mark—clearly a reference to *JG. v. Samford* (1594) also known as *Samforth's Case.* Unfortunately, the plaintiffs failed to prove the amount of their damages, so they were only awarded one shilling. Lauriat (2024) also notes three other successful passing off cases in the latter eighteenth century that were reported only in the popular press. She suggests there probably were more cases during this period than previously recognized.

Just as guild marks were often illegally imitated, so too were makers' marks leading to diminution of their value as assets (Belfante, 2017, 1130–1131; Maite, 2009, 10). Printers complained about rivals imitating their marks as early as 1518 but did so in their publications to inform their customers. Robertson (1869, 415) describes one such complaint that some Florentine printers were imitating the complainant's well-known sign of a dolphin wound round an anchor but with the dolphin's head facing left instead of right. The complaint described this as an "impudent fraud." Richards (2022, 85) notes that the first ever toothpaste ad, published in 1660, cautioned "beware of counterfeits."

One merchant industry active in attacking counterfeits was proprietary medicines. Product sales were particularly robust during the 1643 typhus epidemic in England and the 1665 Great Plague in London (Richards, 2022, 90). The Venetian Republic also saw mark registrations for medicinal products. Heavily advertised proprietary medicines with unique packaging sought direct purchase by consumers as opposed to generic medicines sold by apothecaries and pharmacists. They also sought to prevent counterfeiting by promoting a specific product appearance—changing it to stay ahead of counterfeiters, warning consumers against imitations telling them how to recognize the genuine product and hiring solicitors to locate and threaten imitators (Belfanti, 2017, 1134–1138; Petty, 2019). However, courts were often reluctant to grant trademark protection to such disreputable products. Consistent with this ambivalence, in 1783 Lord Mansfield held there was no property right in the name of a medicine—Dr. Johnson's Yellow Ointment, but it would still constitute fraud if other merchants used that name without permission (Robertson, 1869, 415; *Singleton v. Bolton*, 1783).

THE EIGHTEENTH CENTURY: FIGHTING IMITATION

Richards (2022, 87–97) reports that most print advertising in the 1700s was for books with proprietary medicines in second place. During this century, U.S. newspapers (1704), and magazines (1741) were founded and soon after they began selling advertising space (Sivulka, 1998, 26–27). At this time most advertisements did not include a brand name but rather identified the offering merchant. For example, tobacco and snuff were offered by Peter and George Lorillard in 1789. Lorillard became the name of the company name that by the nineteenth century had created several brand names for cigarettes including the popular Old Gold brand. In many other cases, the merchant's name would later become the brand name.

Lack of judicial enforcement does not mean counterfeiting was not condemned. Merchants continued to warn customers to avoid forgeries. Schechter (1925, 119) reports that in the early 1700s, one London cutler ran newspaper ads describing his particular mark and urging customers to avoid counterfeits. Later a grocer, who used a beehive on his store sign, saw others using similar pictures and ran newspaper ads proclaiming he was the sole proprietor of the original and celebrated beehive. A shop keeper using a grasshopper image on his sign was also imitated and ran similar newspaper notices. However, he was later persuaded to license the grasshopper image to grocers willing to pay (Robertson, 1869, 415).

As noted, marks by this time had become clear assets that were sometimes sold or inherited, but without promotion of the value of the genuine mark/brand in the newspaper notices or elsewhere, it is not clear that brand marketing was commonly practiced during this period even as marks/brands gained a reputation for quality through use of the products and word of mouth.

In the 1700s, British colonies that would become the U.S. also sought protection from product counterfeits. Anecdotal evidence indicates that some courts accepted trade name registrations even before the U.S. was formed. For example, in 1772, a Fairfax Virginia court accepted registration of the mark "G. Washington" for flour (Trademark Reporter, 1992). However, comprehensive state registration laws would not be enacted until 1863.

Such colonial laws requiring identification markings on particular goods such as tobacco and flour were likely continued by states after the adoption of the Constitution. The purpose was to allow purchasers to track product quality to the responsible producer, not enable product promotion by brand name. After the country was formed, a Boston sailmaker petitioned to be allowed to register his trademark with the new federal government and his petition was sent to George Washington's Secretary of State—Thomas Jefferson. Jefferson recommended a statute be passed to provide for trademark registration, but his recommendation was not adopted (Rogers, 1910, 41). That would come a century later.

Similarly, a Philadelphia businessman complained to a Boston newspaper in 1791 about limited damage awards and no injunctions available from the courts:

> [W] hen a person thus injured [by trademark infringement], discovers and brings to publick notice the aggressor, he can obtain no redress adequate to the magnitude of the injury he has sustained, although he may go to an enormous expense and deal of trouble in the business, as well as a waste of time, and after all is perhaps allowed by a jury, moderate damages by no means equivalent to the loss sustained, much less does it prove a salutary remedy against future offences of the like nature. (Schechter, 1925, 133)

CASE STUDY: JOSIAH WEDGEWOOD

The eighteenth century also saw one of the clearest examples of modern brand marketing in the offering of Wedgewood pottery. Josiah Wedgewood was born in Staffordshire, England in 1730. His father was a mediocre potter whose wares were sold predominantly in Staffordshire. Josiah followed his father into the family business but by the 1750s, Josiah made most of his sales in London. He set up his own business in 1759 and organized his factory toward job specialization to ensure consistent quality. He developed numerous innovations including green glaze, creamware, jasper, and black basalt and numerous new product ideas and designs including jasper cameos and tea trays. Wedgewood met Thomas Bentley in 1762. They began working together and became formal partners in 1769. In the early 1770s, they were the first pottery firm to adopt neoclassic images for its products, leading that shift in pottery fashion. However, all these innovations were easily copied.

At this time Wedgewood became one of the first potters to put his name on his products. He impressed his name on the unfired clay making his products more difficult to imitate. Although it was common at this time for many advertised products to promote a person's name who was the producer or seller, Wedgewood became one of the few luxury brands at the time to be known by the manufacturer's name (Koehn, 2001, 33). What distinguished Wedgewood from his rivals was his commitment to creating a luxury brand. He charged high prices (after an initial first-order discount) and pursued upper-class usage to make his wares fashionable and in demand by members of many classes.

He noted that "Fashion is infinitely superior to merit" (McKendrick et al., 1982, 141). In other words, he preferred to promote his brand image of "fashionability" over the functionality of his products. Since members of the Royal family were the epitome of fashion endorsing many types of products, Wedgewood successfully became Potter to the Queen and various members of the Royal family. He then pursued the nobility and gentry. He followed similar strategies in other countries both in Europe and farther afield.

Except for handbills that Wedgewood disdained for being used by common merchants, Wedgewood used various forms of advertising and sales promotion. As noted above, he emphasized his brand name and the brand's "fashionability." McKendrick et al. (1982, 124) note that Wedgwood writes to his then partner Thomas Bentley in 1773 that it was "absolutely necessary" that they mark their goods and that they "advertise the mark." If subsequent advertising (and other promotion) focused on the brand identity evidenced by the Wedgwood & Bentley circular mark, this would appear to be brand marketing even though the brand identifier consists of personal names written within a circle that they used from 1769 to 1781 and pictured below (Fig. 3.2).

Fig. 3.2 Wedgewood and Bentley marks from https://www.antique-hq.com/wedgwood-markings-2434/

Alternatively, Wedgwood could have been insisting that the mark be advertised only to educate consumers to avoid counterfeits. This still would be promotion of the brand identifier but not the development of an abstract brand personality beyond genuineness. In addition, Wedgwood obtained a sort of celebrity status so it is difficult to distinguish promotion of what today would be called his personal brand from promotion of the pottery brand. Given his overall approach, it is most likely he was seeking to create a high-priced luxury brand to appeal to upper- and middle-class consumers. This is one of the earliest examples of modern brand marketing to develop consumer demand for the brand.

REFERENCES

Barron, O. (1911). Heraldry. *Encyclopædia Britannica, 13*(11th ed., pp. 311–330).

Belfanti, C. M. (2017). Branding Before the Brand: Marks, Imitations and Counterfeits in Pre-modern Europe. *Business History, 60*(8), 1127–1146. https://doi.org/10.1080/00076791.2017.1282946

Berg, M., & Clifford, H. (2007). Selling Consumption in the Eighteenth Century: Advertising and the Trade Card in Britain and France. *Cultural and Social History, 4*(2), 145–170.

Blanchard v. Hill (1742). 2 Atk. 484.

Dawson, N. (2003). English Trade Mark Law in the Eighteenth Century: *Blanchard v. Hill* Revisited—Another '*Case of Monopolies*'? *Legal History, 24*(2), 111–142.

Fox-Davies, A. C. (1909). *A Complete Guide to Heraldry.* T.C. & E.C. Jack.

Hulme, E. W. (1896, April). The History of the Patent System Under the Prerogative and at Common Law. *Law Quarterly Review, 46*, 141–154.

JG. v. Samford. (1594). In J. Baker (Ed.), *Baker and Milsom, Sources of English Legal History—Private Law to 1750* (2nd ed. 2010, pp. 673–676). Oxford University Press.

Koehn, N. F. (2001). *Brand New: How Entrepreneurs Earned Consumers' Trust from Wedgwood to Dell.* Harvard Business School Press.

Lauriat, B. (2024). Robinson & Roberts v. Wheble (1771): A New "First" Trademark Case at Common Law. *Law & History Review, 7*, 1–2. Retrieved Accessed May 30, 2024, from https://lawandhistoryreview.org/article/barbara-lauriat-a-first-case-at-common-law/

Maitte, C. (2009). Labels, Brands, and Market Integration in the Modern Era. *Business and Economic History On-Line, 7*, 1–16. https://thebhc.org/sites/default/files/maitte.pdf

McKendrick, N., Brewer, J., & Plumb, J. H. (1982). *The Birth of a Consumer Society: The Commercialization of Eighteenth-Century England.* Indiana University Press.

Mollerup, P. (2013). *Marks of Excellence: The History and Taxonomy of Trademarks.* Phaidon Press.

Petty, R. D. (2019). PAIN-KILLER: A 19th Century Global Patent Medicine and the Beginnings of Modern Brand Marketing. *Journal of Macromarketing, 39*(3), 287–303.

Richards, J. I. (2022). *A History of Advertising: The First 300,000 Years.* Bowman & Littlefield.

Robertson, W. W. (1869, April 23). On Trade Marks. *Journal of the Society of Arts, 14*, 414–417.

Robinson and Roberts v. Wheble. (1771, July). In "Home News," *The Lady's Magazine* (Wheble), 54.

Rogers, E. S. (1910). Some Historical Matter Concerning Trade-Marks. *Michigan Law Review, 9*(1), 29–43.

Rylands, J. P. (1910). Merchants' Marks and Other Medieval Personal Marks. *Transactions of the Historic Society of Lancashire and Cheshire, 62*, 1–34. Retrieved May 31, 2024, from https://www.hslc.org.uk/wp-content/uploads/2017/06/62-2-Rylands.pdf

Schechter, F. I. (1925). *The Historical Foundation of the Law Relating to Trade-Marks.* Columbia University Press.

Singleton v. Bolton (1783). 99 Eng. Rep. 661; 3 Doug. 293 (K.B.).

Sivulka, J. (1998). *Soap, Sex, and Cigarettes: A Cultural History of Advertising.* Wadsworth Publishing Co.

Trademark Reporter. (1992, September–October). Trademark Timeline. *Trademark Reporter, 82,* 1022–1040.

CHAPTER 4

Nineteenth-Century Demand for Brand Protection

Abstract Brand protection and trademark law emerged in the nineteenth century. Courts recognized the validity of trademarks but still showed some reluctance to enforce them against unauthorized imitations.

Keywords Trademark emergence · Early trademark decisions · Smith Brothers

INTRODUCTION

Laird (1998, 17) suggests that in the early 1800s, consumers in the U.S. and Europe selected items for purchase based on inspection and merchant reputations rather than by brand name. Many firms continued Wedgewood's (and others') ongoing practice of using the manufacturer or merchant name to identify product offerings, e.g., Cadbury chocolate (1824), Warren's blacking (1830), Colt's revolver (1835), Proctor & Gamble soaps (1837), Goodyear tires, (1839), Beecham's pills (1842), Babbitt's soap (1851), Studebaker wagons (1852), Smith Brother's cough candies (1852), Levi Strauss denim pants (1853), Mason's jars (1858) (Richards, 2022, 105; Sivulka, 1998, 37). This common practice arguably is the beginning of modern brand marketing.

R. D. Petty, *From Marking Products to Marketing Brands*, Palgrave Studies in Marketing, Organizations and Society, https://doi.org/10.1007/978-3-031-76778-4_4

At this time, Europe began abolishing obligatory labels and certifications on various goods causing demand for legal sanctions against counterfeits. For example, in France after abolishing trade guilds in 1791, a resurgence in counterfeiting occurred causing the government to enact specific prohibitions of counterfeiting in the jewelry, plates, and cutlery industries. Then in 1803 France enacted a criminal statute making it illegal to misrepresent someone else's mark as your own. This statute specifically condemned labeling that claimed the product was "in the style of" a particular merchant or city. The law's sponsor argued it would condemn not only cloth labeled "in the style of" but also from a street or house with the same name as a protected brand. This change was significant because previously such claims if true were deemed non-fraudulent in many jurisdictions including France (Maitte, 2009, 6–8; Richards, 2022, 104).

For the most part, UK guild laws continued to protect marks during the early 1800s. By the 1875 trademark registration act, many marks in guild industries were claiming they had been in use for fifty to over one hundred years prior to that date (Higgins, 2012, 266–267). Individual English marks in some industries tended to be quite like the guild marks and each other. Since merchants were familiar with these subtle differences, such marks were likely used administratively to track wares rather than as brand markings for consumer recognition. This similarity among marks created problems in determining whether marks were too similar to one another to both be registered in the same industry (Higgins, 2012, 279–282).

THE EMERGENCE OF TRADEMARKS

During the early nineteenth century, British court decisions began to develop more consistency in restricting the unauthorized imitation of trademarks. Following the reasoning of early court decisions such as *Blanchard v. Hill* (1742) and *Singleton v. Bolton* (1783), discussed in the previous chapter, an 1824 UK decision that found liability for the intentional counterfeiting of marks. Later, an 1839 Chancery court decision held that intent to deceive need not be proven to obtain injunctive relief (Bently, 2008, 6–7). Bodley (1882, 152) counted fourteen trademark cases before 1825 in Great Britain, Ireland, and America. Duguid (2009, 11–13) indicates that by the 1850s, trademark-related court decisions were reported and followed internationally.

These court decisions also were carefully analyzed. One commentator explained how the addition of one word could in some cases avoid consumer confusion and therefore liability for infringement, e.g., Truefitt's Medicated Mexican Balm does not infringe Perry's Medicated Mexican Balm. However, in other cases adding a single insignificant word may still cause confusion and infringement, e.g., "London Conveyance Company" compared with London Conveyance for Company). Furthermore, the addition of a significant single word could make the remainder of the trademark non-distinctive or generic and available to all rivals to use such as with the Medicated Mexican Balm example above (T.T., 1850, 225).

Not until 1862 did the UK passed its Merchandise Mark Act making it a misdemeanor to forge or counterfeit any trademark with intent to defraud. The act was criticized because intent to defraud is difficult to prove but it was praised because trademarks were broadly defined as any word or device, etc. used to denote the producer or seller of specified goods. Shortly after the Act was passed, judicial decisions announced that the trademark right to exclusive use on particular goods was a property right even though it did not apply to use on completely different products (Robertson, 1869, 415–416).

The U.S., statutory condemnation of trademark counterfeiting began even earlier. In 1845, New York adopted the first state criminal statute that declared counterfeiting "any representation, likeness or similitude, copy or imitation of the private stamp, wrapper or label" affixed on goods to be a criminal misdemeanor punishable by fine or imprisonment (Upton, 1860, 247). Similar statutes were enacted in Connecticut and Pennsylvania in 1847. By 1850, these state criminal statutes started explicitly covering trademarks and brands in addition to labels and stamps (United States Congress, 1900, 91–92). Upton (1860, 247–248) could not recall seeing any prosecutions under these statutes, but they continued to be enacted to number about a dozen by 1900 (United States Congress, 1900, 91–92). Perhaps the threat of possible prosecution was sufficient to persuade infringers to "cease and desist."

U.S. JUDICIAL RECOGNITION OF TRADEMARKS

The first explicit mention of trademarks in US court decisions occurred in the mid-1840s in cases involving brands of thread from Great Britain whose spools and labels were imitated by US companies. The first set of cases involved a Massachusetts company that began imitating the British product, "Taylor's Persian Thread" and selling it in New York City. In October 1844 the Federal Circuit Court of the District of Massachusetts New York Chancery Court issued a short decision enjoining this practice without mentioning trademarks (*Taylor v. Carpenter*, 1844).

A trial then took place and the court's 1846 opinion denying the motion for a new trial repeatedly mentioned "marks." One defense that was raised in this case was that it was customary for businesses to imitate trademarks that were used by foreign companies. This was asserted to be a widespread practice in several countries for at least the past 20 years. The court rejected this assertion that commonplace wrongful usage of another's trademark somehow made the usage legal (*Taylor v. Carpenter*, 1846).

Meanwhile, a New York Chancery Court December 1844 decision in a case between the two same parties also issued an injunction but explicitly discussed the pirating of "trade-marks" (*Taylor v. Carpenter*, 1844). A similar New York Chancery Court decision in 1845 in another British tread case also enjoined the practice of trademark and label infringement while explicitly discussing marks and trademarks. This decision also notes the consistency of its ruling with the newly enacted 1845 New York label counterfeiting statute (*Coats v. Holbrook*, 1845). In the space of a couple of years, court decisions went from not mentioning trademarks to freely discussing them.

The recognition of the concept of trademarks in the second half of the 1840s did not automatically mean that trademark considerations rose above packaging. In 1840, a court dismissed the complaint between two competing newspapers with similar names because the appearance of the two was so dissimilar that confusion was unlikely (*Bell v. Locke*, 1840). Nevertheless an 1849 court decision cited *Bell* for the proposition that "fraudulent use of a mark was a ground for relief" (*Coffeen v. Brunton*, 1849). Seven years after *Bell* in *Partridge v. Menck* (1847), the court affirmed the chancellor's decision to overturn a previous decision to issue an injunction. The court recognized the importance of preventing the pirating of another's goodwill that had built up in a label or trademark but ultimately decided the packaging differences made confusion unlikely. This suggests that while trademarks had become important, they are not more important than the overall appearance of labels and packaging at this time.

As with British court decisions, these 1840s American court decisions led to scholarly examination of trademark law. Francis Upton's path-breaking: *A Treatise on the Law of Trade Marks* (1860) acknowledged that trademark law had become an area of interest and importance in the past quarter of a century. Two scholars counted early U.S. trademark court decisions. Cox (1871) counted 77 distinct court cases up to 1870, some of which had multiple decisions (e.g., trial court and then appellate court). Rogers (1914, 48–49) only counted a total of 62 court decisions up to 1870.

One reason for the discrepancy between these tallies of judicial decisions is that the earliest cases did not mention trademarks by name. Cox's first case was an 1825 decision by the New York (state) Chancery court that refused to issue an injunction against the New York National Advocate newspaper for using the "National Advocate" while noting it was published in New York. The decision noted one name was nearly identical to the other but held there were limited differences between the two names. Furthermore, readers of the original paper were clearly being asked to subscribe to a second paper so that consumers would not be deceived into thinking they were the same newspaper.

Cox's second decision and the first counted by Rogers was an 1837 Massachusetts Supreme Judicial Court decision overturning a jury verdict in a case involving a "patent" medicine. Reminiscent of *Singleton v. Bolton* (1783), this decision discussed whether the words "Thomsonian Medicines" indicated a single source of the product or was a generic description of a type of medicine. Although Samuel Thomson acquired a patent on his medical procedures that he licensed to people for $20 in 1813, the court held that without a patent on this medicine, the plaintiff was not entitled to exclusive rights to sell this product nor exclusive rights to the name "Thomsonian Medicine" if the latter had acquired a generic meaning. The Thomsonian medical movement was quite popular at this time. The court ordered a new trial to determine genericness, but no further proceedings were recorded (*Thomson v. Winchester*, 1837). Samuel Thomson died in 1843 but alternative herbal medicine continues today.

JUDICIAL RELUCTANCE TO PROTECT AGAINST IMITATION

These examples suggest that U.S. courts were not always sympathetic to brand marketers in these early 1800s cases. Despite similar names, dissimilar appearance was found to make trade diversion unlikely. A few early English cases and at least one US decision required trademarks to explicitly identify the manufacturer and would not enforce rights to arbitrary or fanciful names that did not. A few US decisions refused to get involved in disputes between sellers of "quack medicines" and other decisions attempted to distinguish trademarks from generic names and quality indications. Some courts condemned fanciful names as deceptive whereas others were more troubled by their brazen imitation holding that the fact that the original name was fanciful did not excuse imitation (Upton, 1860). The results of the 74 judicial cases from 1845 to 1870 are summarized in the chart below. Of the entire 77 cases, the plaintiff marketer obtained some relief in 45 (nearly 60%) of them (Petty, 2011, 151) (Fig. 4.1).

In 1871, the US Supreme Court recognized the harm of trademark infringement:

> [I]n all cases where rights to the exclusive use of a trade-mark are invaded, it is invariably held that the essence of the wrong consists in the sale of the goods of one manufacturer or vendor as those of another; and that it is only when this false representation is directly or indirectly made that the party who appeals to a court of equity can have relief. This is the doctrine of all the authorities. (*Canal Co v. Clark*, 1871, 322–323)

Thus, the Supreme Court appeared to recognize that protection against imitation of source identifiers was important to avoid injury to purchasers.

However, this quoted decision involved the sale of "Lackawanna Coal" so that no label or packaging was involved. In addition, despite the pro-trademark language quoted above, the Court found the term to be

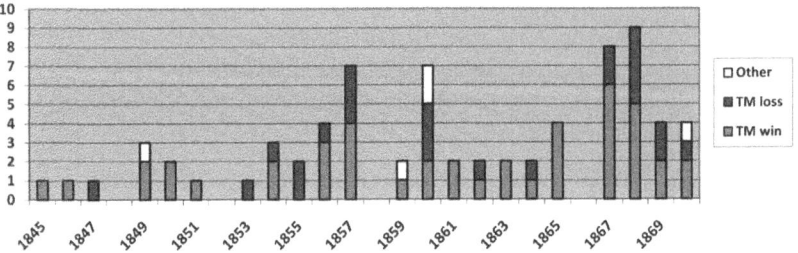

Fig. 4.1 U.S. Trademark Court Decisions 1845–1870 from Petty (2011, 153)

geographically descriptive and therefore not a valid trademark. Nevertheless, it appears by this time the concept of trademark infringement had obtained preeminence over the broader concept of passing off through confusingly similar appearance. The latter would be reserved for cases involving descriptive names that were not entitled to trademark protection (Petty, 2011).

Before leaving this analysis of early court cases, it is worth noting the industries involved. Of Cox's (1871) 77 pre-1870 cases, eleven involved medicinal products with another ten involving personal care items including hair preparations, perfumes, and cosmetics. Ten cases also involved thread or cloth products with another one involving sewing needles. Retail cases, often hotels, accounted for nine cases and newspapers and alcoholic beverages each amounted to five cases. Thus, again anecdotal legal evidence suggests that marketers other than those of patent medicines and tobacco also were interested in protecting their brand identities. Most of these decisions outside the retail category also did not involve simple name similarity but also passing off through the imitation of labels, packaging, and even product instructions.

CASE STUDY: SMITH BROTHERS COUGH DROPS

In 1847, James Smith opened a restaurant/candy store in Poughkeepsie, New York. Around the same time a traveling peddler reportedly named Sly Hawkins offered James the formula for a "cough candy" in exchange for a meal. James accepted the offer and soon was making this candy in his kitchen and selling it in his restaurant. Since he was busy as the cook, it fell to his two sons, William and Andrew, to promote and sell the candy outside the restaurant. This they did in an ever-increasing sales territory. In later litigation, the brothers would claim they spent $5,000 introducing this new product to market.

In early 1852, James Smith & Sons ran a newspaper advertisement in a local newspaper for their "Compound of Wild Cherry Cough Candy" proclaiming it would cure coughs, colds, and other conditions. By December of that year William Smith ran another newspaper advertisement for the "Cough Candy" including a listing of dealers and offering of a liberal price discount to future dealers. Thus, the Smith Brothers sold to dealers much like a traditional manufacturer selling a generic product. But they also promoted their brand to consumers. This shift from generic wholesaling to consumer brand promotion was part of a broader movement in the U.S. at this time (Strasser, 1989, 29–57).

When their father died in 1866, his sons continued the restaurant but devoted most of their time and effort to the cough candy business under the name *Smith Brothers*. Successful consumer branding inevitably led to imitation by similar brands such as the "Schmitt Brothers" or "Smythe Sisters." To combat these imitators, the brothers developed glass display jars for general stores and apothecaries reminiscent of old bulk packaging but with labels containing the name Smith Brother's, the initials S.B., the new product name "cough drops," and portraits of the two brothers. The jars were accompanied by take-home envelopes with the same information. The Quaker Oats company did not start to use its famous portrait of a Quaker gentleman until 1878.

Unfortunately, this did not resolve the imitation problem because unscrupulous retailers simply refilled their glass jars with cheap imitation cough drops. Even molding the initials S.B. on each drop did not solve this problem. Finally, in 1872, the brothers began selling branded, pre-packaged boxes (Cross, 2002, 37–38; Munsey, 2005, 74).

The brothers appear well-advised regarding trademark law. The descriptive name Smith Brothers would not be protectable against similar family names. The term cough drops arguably identified the generic product name and could be used by all firms producing this product. However, the initials S.B. had no meaning by themselves and could be protected. So could their unique portraits (Gorman, 2017). The glass jar and sealed box are pictured below including the drops stamped with S.B. (Munsey, 2005, 74–5). (Fig. 4.2).

When Andrew died in 1884, William inherited his brother's share of the business and continued using the Smith Brothers brand (Munsey, 2005, 73). William obtained two federal trademark registrations in the early 1900s. No. 20,907 was registered in March 1892 and its "essential feature" was the two portraits of the brothers. No. 22,294 was registered in January 1893 and its "essential feature" was the letters "S.B." The descriptions in both registrations also included less protectable features such as the name "Smith Brothers," the words "cough drops," "Poughkeepsie, N.Y.," and the fact that "S.B." was "stamped on every drop." The single image used in both registrations is presented in the advertisement Fig. 4.3.

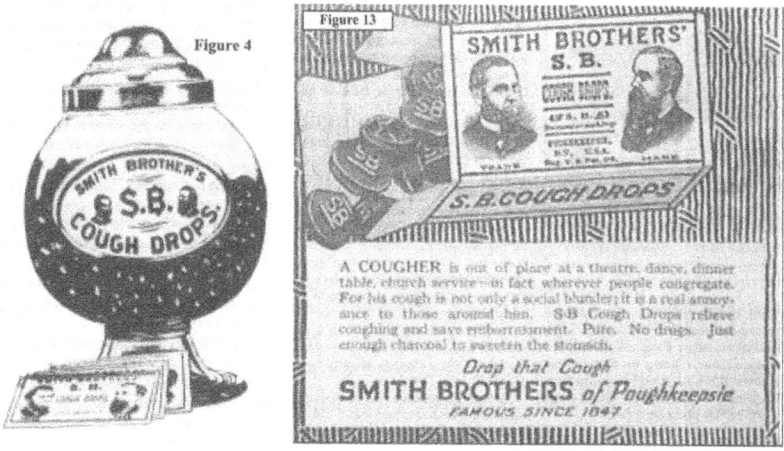

Fig. 4.2   Smith Brothers' Glass Jar and Box from Munsey (2005, 74–75).

Fig. 4.3   Smith Brothers' advertisement from Munsey (2005, 75).

It should be noted that the split of "trade" and "mark" and placement beneath the portraits led to the long-standing story that William was often referred to as "Trade" and Andrew was called "Mark."

The brothers appear to have been well counseled when they developed their trademarks. Their 1892 portrait trademark appears to be one of the earliest portraits registered. A search of the U.S. Patent and Trademark Office database reveals their 1906 portrait registration as the oldest portrait mark in the modern database.

As the table below indicates, the brothers first sued to enforce their unregistered trademark rights in 1882 before their federal trademark registrations. While registration of these trademarks put competitors on notice as to what the Smith Brothers (and the U.S. trademark office) would claim were the protected features of their trademarks, the brothers also were prepared to enforce their rights by litigation if necessary. They filed nine more lawsuits between 1893 and 1895 in various states. They sued for similar brand names, packaging, and the use of two portraits or two initials on packaging.

Accused	Infringing mark	Location	
J. Lutted Co. & Oscar Gemmer	S.P	NY 1882	Enjoined from using S.P. or similar letters and awarded costs of $75
Thomas & Albert Candy	T.C	IL 1893	Enjoined from using similar packaging/ trademarks calculated to deceive ordinary consumers
Vary & Neff	Smyth Brothers S.B. Cough Syrup	IL 1893	Same as above
George Schuster	Schmidt Brothers S.C. Cough Drops+portraits, stamped on each box	OH-	Enjoined from using SC or imitating names, marks, and packages; damages agreed upon
William & George Smith	S.B.+portraits	MD-	Enjoined from using S.B. & similar packaging/trademarks including portraits calculated to deceive ordinary consumers; damages agreed upon

(continued)

(continued)

Accused	Infringing mark	Location	
Sophia Baquol	Not specified	MD 1894	Enjoined from imitating drops, lettering, or packaging calculated to deceive incautious persons; damages agreed upon
Peres & Mendelsohn	P. & M.+portraits	IL 1894	Enjoined from imitating lettering, boxes calculated to deceive incautious persons; infringing boxes to be destroyed
Schwarz & Schwarz	Schwarz & Sons "S" Cough Drops+stamped on each drop	NJ 1894	Enjoined from using boxes calculated to deceive incautious persons but otherwise can sell Smith Bros. cough drops; damages agreed upon
Bird Brothers	B.B.+portraits, stamped on each drop, and trademark	MA 1894	Enjoined from using boxes or lettering calculated to deceive incautious persons but otherwise can use their names; damages agreed upon
Hero & Hero	Dr. H & s's New Champion Cough Drop+portraits	MA 1895	Enjoined from imitating lettering, boxes calculated to deceive incautious persons; agreed to nominal damages of $1

Their most extensive set of legal disputes were against a Buffalo, N.Y. firm known as Burt & Sindele who claimed to be the sellers of the "original cough B. & S. drops" since 1891. William Smith sued Burt & Sindele in 1895 seeking both an injunction and damages in U.S. Circuit Court. Initially, he was awarded a preliminary injunction, but that decision was reversed upon appeal and the case was dismissed in February 1896. The court held that alleging two initials infringing on the S.B. trademark was insufficient without more examination of the circumstances of use such as type style, position on the product, etc. (*Burt v. Smith*, 1896).

Burt then decided to sue for malicious prosecution seeking damages from when the injunction was in effect. The New York State trial court held the plaintiff failed to prove a lack of probable cause in bringing the lawsuit and ordered dismissal. The appellate court reversed but the Court of Appeals, the highest court in New York State, reversed affirming the decision of the trial court to dismiss the case. The vacating of the preliminary injunction did not by itself prove bad faith to establish malicious prosecution. This dismissal was affirmed by the U.S. Supreme Court (*Burt v. Smith*, 1905). A decade of litigation was finally over.

At its peak, the Smith Brothers produced about one million packages per day. Eventually, the family sold the company to Warner-Lambert in 1964. Warner-Lambert closed the Poughkeepsie factory in 1972 and sold the firm to F&F Foods of Chicago in 1977 (Levine, 2014). The brand was acquired by Lanes Brands in 2016 and the cough drops are still being sold today using the brother's portraits and nicknames.

REFERENCES

Bell v. Locke (1840), 8 Paige Ch. 75 (Chancery Court of New York).

Bently, L. (2008). The Making of Modern Trade Mark Law: The Construction of the Legal Concept of Trademark. In L. Bently, J. Davis, & J. C. Ginsburg (Eds.), *Trademarks and Brands: An Interdisciplinary Critique* (pp. 3–14). Cambridge University Press.

Blanchard v. Hill (1742). 2 Atk. 484.

Bodley, T. (1882). What Is a Trademark? *The Kentucky Law Journal, 2*(1), 151–156.

Burt v. Smith. (1896). 71 Federal Reporter 161 (Circuit Court of Appeals, Second Circuit).

Burt v. Smith. (1905). 73 N.E. 495, 181 N.Y. 1 (New York Court of Appeals), *Appeal Dismissed*, 203 U.S. 129 (1906).

Canal Co v. Clark (1871). 80 U.S. 311.

Coats v. Holbrook (1845). 2 Sand. Ch. 586 (Chancery Court of New York).

Coffeen v. Brunton (1849). 5 F. Cas. 1184 (Circuit Court District of Indiana), motion for rehearing to dissolve the preliminary injunction denied. 5 F. Cas. 1186.

Cox, R. (Ed.), (1871). *American Trade Mark Cases; a Compilation of All the Reported Trade Mark Cases Decided in the American Courts Prior to the Year 1871*. R. Clarke & Co.

Cross, M. (2002). *A Century of American Icons*. Greenwood Press.

Duguid, P. (2009). French Connections: The International Propagation of Trademarks in the Nineteenth Century. *Enterprise & Society, 10*(1), 3–37.

Gorman, C. (2017). The Role of Trademark Law in the History of US Visual Identity Design, c.1860–1960. *Journal of Design History, 30*(4), 371–388. https://www.jstor.org/stable/48545556

Higgins, D. M. (2012). Forgotten Heroes and Forgotten Issues: Business and trademark History During the Nineteenth Century. *Business History Review, 86*(2), 261–285.

Laird, P. W. (1998). *Advertising Progress: American Business and the Rise of Consumer Marketing*. The Johns Hopkins University Press.

Levine, D. (2014). A Behind-the-Scenes Look at Poughkeepsie's Cough Drop History. https://hvmag.com/life-style/a-behind-the-scenes-look-at-poughkeepsies-cough-drop-history/

Maitte, C. (2009). Labels, Brands, and Market Integration in the Modern Era. *Business and Economic History On-Line, 7*, 1–16. https://thebhc.org/sites/default/files/maitte.pdf

Munsey, C. (2005). Smith Brothers' Cough Drops as a Patent Medicine. *Bottles and Extras* (Summer), 73–76. https://www.fohbc.org/PDF_Files/SmithBros_CMunsey.pdf

Partridge v. Menck (1847). 2 Sand Ch. 622 (Chancery Court of New York), affirmed, 6 Sarat. Ch. Sent. 57 (Supreme Court of New York).

Petty, R. D. (2011). Labels and Trademarks and Prints, Oh My! Legal Evidence of US Interest in Brand Protection in the 1800s. In L. Neilson (Ed.), *Marketing History. In the New World, Proceedings of the 15th Biennial Conference in Historical Analysis & Research in Marketing (CHARM)* (pp. 145–156).

Richards, J. I. (2022). *A History of Advertising: The First 300,000 Years*. Bowman & Littlefield.

Robertson, W. W. (1869, April 23). On Trade Marks. *Journal of the Society of Arts, 14*, 414–417.

Rogers, E. S. (1914). *Good Will, Trade-Marks and Unfair Trading*. A. W. Shaw Co.

Singleton v. Bolton (1783). 99 Eng. Rep. 661; 3 Doug. 293 (K.B.).

Sivulka, J. (1998). *Soap, Sex, and Cigarettes: A Cultural History of Advertising*. Wadsworth Publishing Co.

Strasser, S. (1989). *Satisfaction Guaranteed: The Making of the American Mass Market*. Pantheon Books.

Taylor v. Carpenter (1846). 2 Sand. Ch. 600,604 (N.Y. Ch. 1846).

Taylor v. Carpenter (1844). 11 Paige Ch. 292 (New York Chancery Ct.). and 23 F. Cas. 742 (Circuit Court, District of Massachusetts).

Thomson v. Winchester (1837). 36 Mass. 214 (Massachusetts Supreme Court) and 19 Pick. 214.

United States Congress. (1900). *Report of the Commissioners Appointed to Revise the Statutes Relating to Patents, Trade and Other Marks, and Trade and Commercial Names.* Government Printing Office.

Upton, F. H. (1860). *A Treatise on the Law of Trade Marks.* Weare C. Little Law Bookseller.

CHAPTER 5

U.S. Copyright and Design Patent Registration for Trademarks: 1840–1870

Abstract Building on historical traditions for registering various types of marks with guilds and courts, some marketers filed to register some aspects of their promotional materials as copyrights or design patents when such registrations became available. In the U.S. and probably other countries, these efforts typically were resisted by the government. This chapter examines copyright and design registration from the perspective of marketers seeking to register brand identifiers and is based on Petty 2012a). Registration of trademarks per se is explored in the following chapter.

Keywords Copyright registration · Design patents · Label copyrights Coca-cola bottle

INTRODUCTION

The reduction in guild authority in Europe not only led to judicial and legislative recognition of trademarks but also for proposals to establish trademark registration systems to replace guild registration systems. As shown in the previous chapter, mere use of a particular trademark did not

© The Author(s), under exclusive license to Springer Nature   47
Switzerland AG 2024
R. D. Petty, *From Marking Products to Marketing Brands*, Palgrave
Studies in Marketing, Organizations and Society,
https://doi.org/10.1007/978-3-031-76778-4_5

predictably grant its enforcement in court. Bringing a court challenge was not only risky but also expensive.

Registration of a mark would at least put rivals on notice of the assertion of trademark rights for the mark within a particular industry. It also would provide a minimum first date of use from the application date or from the date of first use as indicated on the application in most systems. A registered trademark has a presumption of validity that might persuade an infringer to "cease and desist" rather than go to trial, particularly if criminal penalties were sought.

Nevertheless, countries appeared reluctant to establish trademark registration systems. In the UK, marketers attempted to register labels as designs after passage of the 1842 Designs Act and then they tried to register labels as copyrights after the 1862 Copyright Act. It wasn't until 1875 that a UK statute authorizing the registration of trademarks was passed (Bently, 2008, 6–10). In the U.S., marketers first attempted to register labels as copyrights and later tried registration as design patents.

U.S. Copyright Registration for Labels: 1830–1870

Congress showed little interest in trademark or label protection in the early 1800s (Petty, 2012a). Some courts continued their colonial practice of accepting name registrations in some industries. This tradition of court registration was continued in the first U.S. copyright statute of 1790. At that time copyright registration was limited to books, maps, and charts. Authors of such works were required to send a copy of their work to the Secretary of State in exchange for a 14-year term of exclusive use with one possible 14-year renewal.

Copyright law was expanded in 1802 to include prints that were designed and engraved, etched, or worked. In addition to depositing these works, a notice of copyright registration had to be included on or in the work and a newspaper notice had to be published. There is no evidence in this early period that U.S. copyright law was used to protect labels, packaging, advertising prints, or trademarks (Petty, 2012a). A perusal of a compilation of copyrighted works through 1821 reveals no titles that appear to be anything other than books, directories, gazetteers, maps, or charts (American Museum, 1822).

After the 1831 copyright amendments simplified registration and extended the term of protection to 28 years with a possible renewal period of 14 years, U.S. marketers began to register labels for copyright protection by the 1840s. They were registered with federal court clerks as prints or engravings or both (Petty, 2012a).

In 1846, the Smithsonian was created and both it and the Library of Congress were supposed to receive copies of copyright registered works. From August 1846 through the end of 1849 there were 46 registrations for Maps, Charts, Prints, and Labels. Only four of these were for commercial labels and all of them for nostrums: "Musury's compound extract of Sarsaparilla and Wau-a-hoo," and three labels from Dr. Stephen Jewett to cover his "Celebrated health resorting bitters," "Highly celebrated pulmonary Elixer," and "Highly and justly celebrated strengthening plaster" (Board of Regents, 1852, 233–236).

In 1850, this category contained an additional 43 entries including the four labels previously registered (they may have been registered in different courts from the prior registrations). In addition, registrations were received for eight other labels all of which appear again to be associated with nostrums: Dr. Moffat's "The Phoenix Bitters" (in French, Spanish and German), "Compound Syrup of Hops and Boneset," "Equarian Condition Powders," "Fahnestock's Vermifuge," "Forsha's Balm Liniment," "Hoffland's celebrated German Bitters," "Jewett & Co.'s Chromolith Card," and "Moffat's celebrated Phoenix Bitters" (Board of Regents, 1852, 322–325). This increase in labels registered in 1850 over the prior three years suggests label registrations were likely increasing at this time. Brand marketers appear to have found value in labels with some image component.

In 1856, the Secretary of State issued a circular to court clerks ordering them to refuse registration of labels. However, court clerks continued registering labels arguing their duty was the ministerial recording of items not their examination for qualification of copyright protection (Rosen, 2023). Copyright Account Books from 1856 to 1864 for the US District Court for the District of Massachusetts (available at the US National Archives ARC Identifier 2945753) identify several prints by apparent product names suggesting these prints were intended as labels.

While many of these entries are for medicines, some were for other consumer products such as flypaper, rat poison, shoe polish, and hair dye. Similarly, a search for labels between 1850 and 1860 yielded 162 results of which 58 could be identified as labels or ads including about 24 for tobacco, 17 for medicine, 8 for liquor, and 13 for miscellaneous products such as sewing machines, coal sifters, bean and legume separators, and furniture as well as disposable products such as cloth, soap, sarsaparilla, gunpowder, and entertainment. Petty (2012a) suggests that labels might account for 10% or more of all copyright registrations at this time. Label protection appears primarily focused on presenting the brand name and protecting unique visual clues.

By midcentury, marketers had come to understand the problem and some marketers began adding artistic images to their labels. Below left and center are two such commercial labels: a hair restorer circa 1838 and an 1846 label for "Infant Cordial." Both are identified by the common practice of using inventor/merchant's name. The seller's name type in these examples is almost as large as the type of the descriptive product name. The development of color printing in the 1870s would make color labels (and other advertising) more feasible in the future as illustrated by the color trade card pictured below right (Fig. 5.1).

Trade cards were developed to be protected by copyright law, to identify a brand, and to associate that brand to the image on the card. Trade cards proved extremely popular with the public and were distributed a large variety of businesses, often in product packaging as a prize or bonus. Color printing was still very much a novelty so the cards were valued for

Fig. 5.1   Labels and a Trade Card from the Library of Congress

their vibrant images. Consumers often collected these cards and traded them with others showing the cards themselves had value beyond identifying a brand. The fad faded by 1900 (Cornell University, 2017; Strasser, 1989, 164–165).

Enforcement Against Registered Labels

Seventeen years after the 1802 act courts were authorized to enjoin unauthorized copying of copyright protected works (Bowker, 1912). But that doesn't mean courts always did so. Strasser (1989, 36) notes that early labels were largely descriptive rather original artistic works usually associated with copyright protection. In 1848, the federal circuit court of Ohio refused to enjoin an imitation of a registered medicine label ("Dr. Rodgers' Compound Syrup of Liverwort and Tar") as copyright infringement.

After examining British judicial precedent, the court held replication of the commercial label did not cause a copyright injury (*Scoville v. Toland*, 1848). The label had no intrinsic value beyond identifying the medicine. It was not intended to be read or bought and sold on its own. The only harm in the case was the fraudulent sale of an imitation medicine. The court decided the copyright statute did not authorize the protection of labels that merely assert a medicine can cure certain diseases and indicate how it should be used. Soon other courts agreed that labels had to contain artistic expression to be protected by copyright law (Rosen, 2012).

Design Patent Registration

In 1841, even as some labels began being registered as copyrights, Patent Commissioner Ellsworth recommended that Congress enact a statute to protect "new and original designs for articles of manufacture, both in the fine and useful arts, to the authors and proprietors thereof." The following year, the statute to protect design patents was enacted to create a seven-year patent protection for new and original (1) designs for products, (2) shapes or configurations of products, (3) impressions or ornaments to be placed on products, (4) patterns, prints, or pictures to be worked or fixed onto products, (5) designs for the printing of fabrics, and (6) designs for sculptures or carvings (Hudson, 1948). Many of these early design patents covered stoves, fireplace, utensils, and clock face designs. The function of an ornamental design is to provide a distinctive aspect of design that is pleasing and attractive (Symons, 1914, 14).

When Patent Commissioner Ellsworth spoke to Congress in 1841 advocating this new law, he stressed that without design protection, manufacturers could freely copy their competitors' designs. Thus, designers had little incentive to invest much of their resources in creating new designs. With protection, Ellsworth argued, the financial incentive would increase design output and quality (Hudson, 1948, 380–81).

Thirty years later in *Gorham Mfg. v. White* (1872, 525, 528), the Supreme Court recognized that design patents could "enhance [the] salable value" and "enlarge the demand" for products. It further noted that design patents would enable firms to distinguish their products from those of their competitors. Judicial interpretation of the design patent statute allowed for new prints, pictures, or ornamental designs to be registered as design patents based on their novelty rather than their ability to identify a distinct source of a product, i.e., functioning as a trademark. Thus, design patents were another early effort to prevent competitors from unfairly imitating a successful rival and mislead consumers to purchase a product other than that they intended to purchase.

TRADEMARKS REGISTERED AS DESIGN PATENTS STARTING IN 1855

Because the copyright protection of labels was put in doubt by the 1850s, the U.S. design patent system began registering designs for labels and trademarks (as well as occasional bottles and containers) during that time. A search of the Annual Reports of the Commissioner of Patents from 1849 through 1854 reveals no trademark designs (Petty, 2012a).

The first patent designated as a "design for trade-mark" appears to be design patent number 725—one of 71 design patents issued in 1855. That year also saw the issuance of design patent number 717—"a design for labels on bottles and jars." This label design might also be a trademark if it was intended to identify a particular source of the product for consumers. Thus, these two design patents may be the first federally registered "trademarks" from a brand marketing perspective. These two potential trademark design patents amount to about 3% of the total design patents issued in 1855. A later design patent (1864) is pictured below and identified as for "Labelling Barrels." It presents the image of whole-some farm workers harvesting wheat to produce whisky and includes the producer's name as well as its purpose of saving the buyer from "worthless imitations" (Fig. 5.2).

It's recognition of "designs as trademarks" in the mid-1850s enabled the U.S. Patent Office, responsible for copyright registrations begin-ning in 1859, to again address copyright protection of trademarks. The Patent Office issued another circular again ordering courts not to register "stamps, labels, and other trade-marks of any manufactured articles,

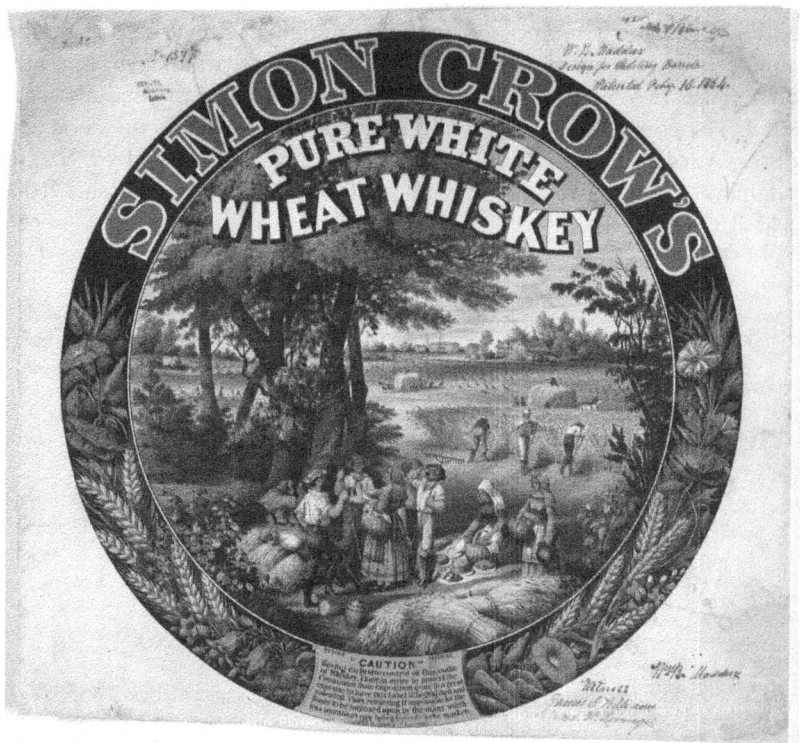

Fig. 5.2 Design Patent (https://s3.amazonaws.com/NARAprodstorage/lz/rediscovery/27501-28000/27572-2015-001-ac.jpg)

goods or merchandise" as copyrights (Rosen, 2023). However as noted above, that did not prevent the court clerk for the federal District Court of the District of Massachusetts from registering trademarks through at least 1864.

Design patents on trademarks, labels, and bottles (including an occasional match box or other container) trickled in until the end of the Civil War as shown by the chart below. 1865 saw 17 purported trademarks registered as design patents out of 221 design patents (8%) and the peak occurred in 1868 when 58 potential trademarks were registered as design patents out of 446 total design patents (13%). Although the number of design patents registered in the next two years increased to 508 (1869) and 737 (1870), the number of potential trademarks registered as design patents decreased to 44 (1869) and 26 (1870). Symons (1912) notes that "some two hundred" design patents for trademark designs were issued. The count here is 202 plus additional design patents on labels and bottles. A total of about 3800 design patents were registered by 1870, so trademarks on designs were only about 0.5% of all design patents from 1842–1870.

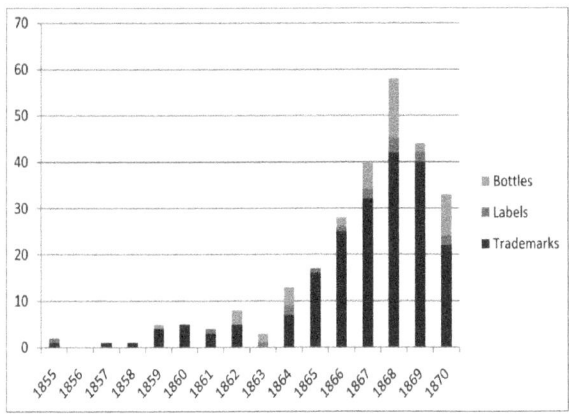

U.S. Design Patent Registrations for Trademarks, Bottles and Labels 1855–1870

While counting the number of design patent trademark registrations is relatively straightforward, identifying the products subject to design patent trademarks is more difficult because the records are unclear (Petty, 2012a). Nonetheless, records indicate that the single design patent (#971) for a trademark registered in 1857 was for plough springs. A second design for that year (#918) was for "Medallions of Franklin to mark Pens and Pen-Holders." Two out of four designs for trademarks in 1859 identify their respective products as soap boxes and "Bragg's Arctic liniment." Similarly, two out of five design trademarks in 1860 identified their products as "S. Armitage's Neuralgic Pills" and lead pencils. In 1862, design trademark industries that were identified included an elixir, a medicine, shoes, and a sword blade.

The 1864 and later reports contained larger numbers of registrations but shorter descriptions generally including only the registrant, assignee if there was one, a vague category such as trademark, bottle or label and the design patent number. Nonetheless a lead pencil trademark was identified in 1865 and again in 1866 and 1868. 1866 also included a trademark for pens and pen boxes.

Thus, this perusal of both design patents and copyright registrations suggests that marketers not only sought some form of brand identity protection but also supported a registration system as the basis for such protection. In addition, the nostrum industry appears to have led the way in developing and registering distinctive names and labels for their products. A smaller group of marketers of various products also applied for registrations but these registrants appear to be exceptions in their industries rather than part of a broader trend. The story of copyright and design patent brand protection continues in the next chapter.

Case Study: The Coca-Cola Bottle

Although this chapter nominally covers the time-period from 1840 to 1870, this case study of the Coca-Cola bottle is placed here because it was famously initially protected from imitation by design patents. Indeed, the classic Coke bottle may be one of the most famous design trademarks in the world. The story of the Coke bottle starts in 1886 when Charles Pemberton invented Coca-Cola as a fountain drink. Coca-Cola was then one of hundreds of "nerve tonics" being offered to American consumers to ease their illnesses and discomforts. The company initially produced Coca-Cola syrup and sold it to soda fountains that sold it by the glass.

In 1891, Asa Candler acquired Coca-Cola and in 1899 he agreed to a perpetual exclusive license with two lawyers from Atlanta to franchise bottlers in most of the U.S. Exceptions were made for territories that already had bottlers producing consumer-sized bottles of Coca-Cola. In that fateful year of 1899, the firm sold 280,000 gallons of syrup—the equivalent of almost 36 million drinks of Coca-Cola. This marked a dramatic increase since 1890 when the firm sold only about 9,000 gallons of syrup. By 1928, sales of bottled syrup exceeded fountain syrup and the number of bottling franchises peaked 1,263 (Pendergrast, 2000, 59–76, 138).

Coke's popularity caused imitators—both among soda fountain vendors and among producers of bottled beverages (Petty, 2012b). To address the latter problem, the company first developed a unique diamond-shaped label in 1906. Unfortunately, bottled coke was often presented for sale in a large bucket of ice where the label would soak off the bottle. A new approach was needed. Design patents on bottle configurations were not unusual by this time.

After much internal discussion, the trustees of the Coca-Cola Bottling Association voted to expend up to $500 to develop a distinctive bottle in April 1915. Eight to ten glass companies soon received a challenge to develop a "bottle so distinct that you would recognize if by feel in the dark or lying broken on the ground." Root Glass won the contest with the somewhat bulky bottle illustrated below. It reportedly was inspired by the cocoa pod (not an ingredient in Coke) after research Coke ingredients coca and kola.

Coke received a design patent on this prototype in November 1915. Unfortunately, this model tipped over easily interfering with the production process, so the prototype was quickly slenderized. While Coke used the slender bottle for production, it did not seek a patent on the new design until 1923 (Gersen & Hemphill, 2023, 366–370). These two design patent drawings are pictured below along with a picture of the bulkier bottle itself. Note neither design patent mentions Coca-Cola in order to keep the applications secret from rivals. (Fig. 5.3).

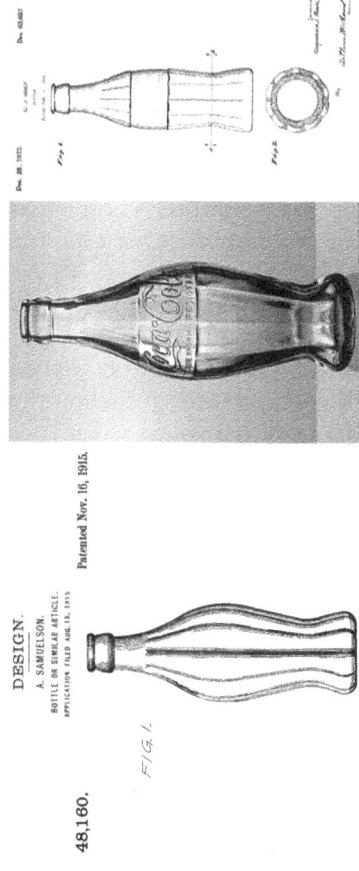

Fig. 5.3   US Patent and Trademark Office

Because Coke did not seek a second design patent until 1923, it had to base infringement cases before that time on the original design patent or on passing off under unfair competition law. Most of its enforcement efforts involved names of various degrees of similarity to Coca-Cola and copying the trademarked script name (U.S. registered trademark in 1893), bottle, label, and even the bottle cap. Since blatant copying appears intentional (rather than coincidence), courts typically condemned it (Gersen & Hemphill, 2023, 374–377; Petty, 2012b, 239).

However, Coca-Cola lost its argument in a 1927 case that the essence of its bottle design was the curving out and then curving in of the bottle. The court found several earlier design patents with the same feature. The court therefore limited Coke's design to symmetry and proportion as well as ornamentation. It found no infringement by a competitor's bottle that was longer rather than stocky with different proportions (*Coca-Cola Co. v. Whistle Co.*, 1927).

The bottle was revised slightly in 1937 and another design patent was registered to Coca-Cola. It is illustrated below left. The design patent expired in 1951 but it was not until Spring 1959 that Coca-Cola applied for a registered trademark for the so-called contour bottle including the name Coca-Cola molded into the glass. The mark was issued a year later (U.S. Trademark registration 696147) and is illustrated below middle. In addition to this bottle trademark that is still in force today, Coke registered the bottle shape with no words in 1977—illustrated below left (U.S. Trademark registration 1057884).

The contour bottle is a classic brand identifier—it is well known by consumers even without any verbal identification of Coca-Cola brand. It harks back to the marking of shipping containers but adds an innovative shape eligible for design patent protection. Coke used decades of design patent protection to heavily advertise the bottle and its distinctive shape. This promotion allowed it to register the bottle shape as a trademark because it indicated the source of the product, the brand, in the minds of consumers. (Fig. 5.4).

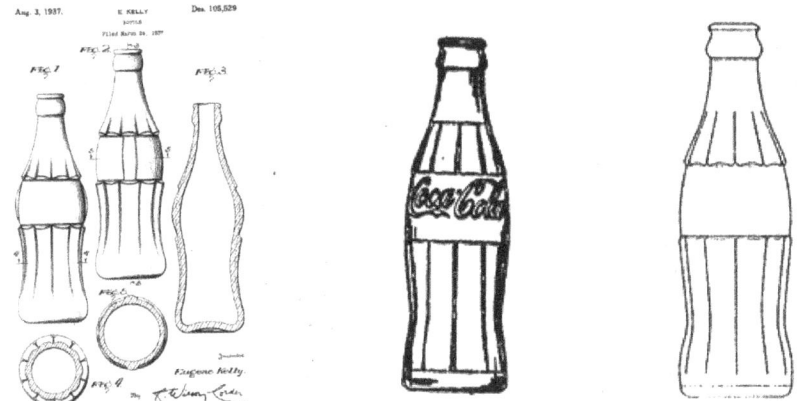

Fig. 5.4 US Patent and Trademark Office

REFERENCES

American museum and repository of arts and sciences. (1822). *American Museum and Repository of Arts and Sciences, as Connected with Domestic Manufactures and National Industry. Also, a List of All the Patents Granted by the United States, Up to the End of Year 1821. With a List of All the Books That Have Been Deposited in the Department of State for Securing Their Copyright According to Law.* J. Milligan.

Bently, L. (2008). The Making of Modern Trade Mark Law: The Construction of the Legal Concept of Trademark. In L. Bently, J. Davis, & J. C. Ginsburg (Eds.), *Trademarks and Brands: An Interdisciplinary Critique* (pp. 3–14). Cambridge University Press.

Board of Regents of the Smithsonian Institution. (1852). *Fifth Annual Report of the Board of Regents of the Smithsonian Institution.* Government Printing Office.

Bowker, R. R. (1912). *Copyright: Its History and Its Law.* Houghton Mifflin Co.

Coca-Cola Co. v. Whistle Co. (1927). 20 F.2d 955 (D. Del.).

Coca-Cola Company. *The History of the Coca-Cola Contour Bottle: The Creation of a Cultural Icon.* Retrieved June 26, 2024, from https://www.coca-colaco mpany.com/about-us/history/the-history-of-the-coca-cola-contour-bottle

Cornell University. (2017). *Trade Cards: An Illustrated History.* https://rmc.lib rary.cornell.edu/tradecards/exhibition/history/index.html#modalClosed

Gersen, J. E., & Hemphill, C. S. (2023). The Coca-Cola Bottle: A Fragile Vessel for Building a Brand. In J. E. Gersen & J. H. Steckel (Eds.), *Legal Applications of Marketing Theory* (pp. 361–383) Cambridge University Press.

Gorham Co. v. White. (1872). 81 U.S. 511–531.

Hudson, T. B. (1948). A Brief History of the Development of Design Patent Protection in the United States. *Journal of the Patent Office Society, 30*(5), 380–400.

Pendergrast, M. (2000). *For God, Country and Coca-Cola: The Definitive History of the Great American Soft Drink and the Company That Makes It*. Perseus Books Group.

Petty, R. D. (2012a). From Label to Trademark: The Legal Origins of the Concept of Brand Identity in Nineteenth Century America. *Journal of Historical Research in Marketing, 4*(1), 129–153.

Petty, R. D. (2012b). Coca-Cola Brand Protection Before World War II—It's the Real Thing! *Journal of Historical Research in Marketing, 4*(2), 224–244.

Rosen, Z. S. (2012). Reimagining Bleistein: Copyright for Advertisements in Historical Perspective. *Journal of the Copyright Society U.S.A., 59*(Winter), 347–389. Retrieved from SSRN: https://ssrn.com/abstract=1507125 or https://doi.org/10.2139/ssrn.1507125

Rosen, Z. S. (2023). Examining Copyright. *Journal of the Copyright Society of the USA, 69*, 481–564. Retrieved from SSRN: https://ssrn.com/abstract=4099976 or https://doi.org/10.2139/ssrn.4099976

Scoville v. Toland (1848), 21 F. Cas. 863 (D. Ohio).

Strasser, S. (1989). *Satisfaction Guaranteed: The Making of the American Mass Market*. Pantheon Books.

Symons, W. L. (1912). Early Attempts to Protect Trademarks. *Scientific American, 106*(16), 33.

Symons, W. L. (1914). *The Law of Patents for Designs*. John Byrne & Co.

CHAPTER 6

Trademark Registration

Abstract National trademark registration systems evolved in the nineteenth century. The U.S. federal system of trademark registration of 1870 was stimulated by both earlier state trademark laws and by international trademark agreements. It pre-empted design patent trademarks but not copyright registration for prints and labels. Examining both the number of registrations over time and the variety of industries involved suggest that brand marketing was increasing during this period.

Keywords Trademark registration · Copyright label registration · Samson Rope Works · Trademark treaties · Trademark design patents · International trademark enforcement

INTRODUCTION

Prior to the nineteenth century, registration systems for marks used in trade operated at the local level on an industry-by-industry basis. As production expanded leading to greater trade at the national and international levels, such systems were too inconvenient and tedious to function efficiently. While some industries continued with their particular registration systems, most converted to national cross-industry systems. The

R. D. Petty, *From Marking Products to Marketing Brands*, Palgrave Studies in Marketing, Organizations and Society, https://doi.org/10.1007/978-3-031-76778-4_6

growing demand for trademark registration also required countries to address how prior systems of design patents and copyright registration would interact with the new systems of trademark registrations.

PRE-1870 STATE REGISTRATION EFFORTS

In 1845, New York enacted the first state trademark statute which was followed by a dozen more states before the federal law of 1870. These statutes varied in coverage from just labels to stamps, trademarks, brands, remedies, etc. They also varied in enforcement (criminal vs private lawsuits) and remedies, e.g., injunctions, fines, damages, but they appear seldom if ever enforced.

In 1863, California enacted a similar statute but added the requirement that trademarks be registered with the state before imitators could be criminally prosecuted. Oregon followed this model in 1864 and Nevada in 1865 (Duguild, 2013; United States Congress, 1900, 91–92). Marketers registered marks hoping to deter imitators bolstered with the threat of possible criminal prosecution. In 1865, a California court held that the new state statute did not preempt common law and equitable remedies (*Derringer v. Plate*, 1865). This allowed private trademark litigation to continue for both unregistered and registered trademarks in that state.

Contrary to the story that nation-wide industrialization in the U.S. stimulated the demand for national trademark registration, registrations in California and other early registration states were primarily from small firms. Of the 151 marks registered in California during the first decade of registration. 83% were from small companies in the medicine, food, drink, alcohol, tobacco, and cosmetic industries (Duguild, 2013, 588–590). It's not clear whether any of these registrations were followed by criminal prosecutions, but this marked the beginning of an international trend in favor of trademark registration.

TRADEMARK REGISTRATION INTERNATIONALLY

Other countries also developed national trademark registration systems at this time. Spain started its trademark registration program in 1850 (Duguid, 2009, 24; Saiz & Perez, 2012). The Spanish system recognized trademarks as property rights but would only grant them to companies, domestic or foreign, with a location in Spain. While some of these foreign trademarks were registered only to protect them against imitation in Spain, Saiz and Perez (2012, 256–257), assert that other marks were registered to enable brand marketing in distant cities, department stores, international exhibitions, and to facilitate magazine advertising.

France started judicial registration in 1803 as a requirement before bringing an enforcement action but it didn't develop a centralized registration system until 1857. As with Spain, registration would be available to domestic and foreign firms if the latter had a location in France. Alternatively, foreign firms whose home country provided reciprocal protection for trademarks of French firms also were eligible to register trademark in France. At the time, the only country with which France enjoyed such a bilateral trade agreement was Russia. But within the next ten years, a dozen countries including the UK signed similar agreements with France and the U.S. followed suit in 1869 (Duguid, 2009).

Portugal started trademark registration in 1883 but within the first two years nearly two-thirds of the registrations were from foreign firms. This figure dropped to 13% by 1905 (Duguid et al., 2010, 26). Ultimately, global firms found their relatively famous trademarks were frequently imitated by local firms in any given country (e.g., Higgins, 2008, 46; Petty, 2012, 136). Indeed, some countries such as Japan and some in Latin America set up registration systems on a first-to-file system so that local firms could control famous foreign trademarks if they registered before the foreign firm (da Silva Lopes & Casson, 2012, 300, 304–305).

To address the usurpation of internationally known trademarks, firms first encouraged their home counties to sign bilateral agreements with their largest foreign markets. These bilateral agreements led to the Paris Convention for the Protection of Industrial Property of 1883 that established the general principle of reciprocity of intellectual property rights so that foreign firms from signatory countries are treated the same as domestic firms in signatory countries. They could register their trademarks in foreign countries just like domestic firms in those countries (Higgins, 2012, 273–274). The 1891 Treaty of Madrid established "one stop" registration for signatory countries allowing firms to register in their home country and include an international registration that was then forwarded to designated other signatory countries (da Silva Lopes & Casson, 2012, 295).

In 1868, the U.S. government negotiated a treaty for the mutual condemnation of trademark counterfeiting with Russia. This treaty was the first authorization for the filing of trademarks, albeit it Russian trademarks, with the Patent Office. Similar treaties with Belgium and France quickly followed.

1870 U.S. Federal Trademark Registration Statute Enacted

Given that foreign trademarks could now be registered with the U.S. Patent Office, it is not surprising that the first trademark registration statute proposal was introduced in Congress in 1869 to put American marketers on equal footing with foreign firms. It passed in 1870 along with revisions of patent and copyright law (Rosen, 2009, 836–840). Pictured below is trademark number one registered to Averill Chemical Paint Company registered its trademark for liquid paint on October 25, 1870. The registered trademark is the circular picture of an eagle standing on the rock of chemistry. While this trademark does not include any sort of creative brand name, it balances information about product performance (economical, durable, and beautiful according to banners held by the eagle) with a strong brand image of the eagle perched on chemistry that is depicted as a rock (Fig. 6.1).

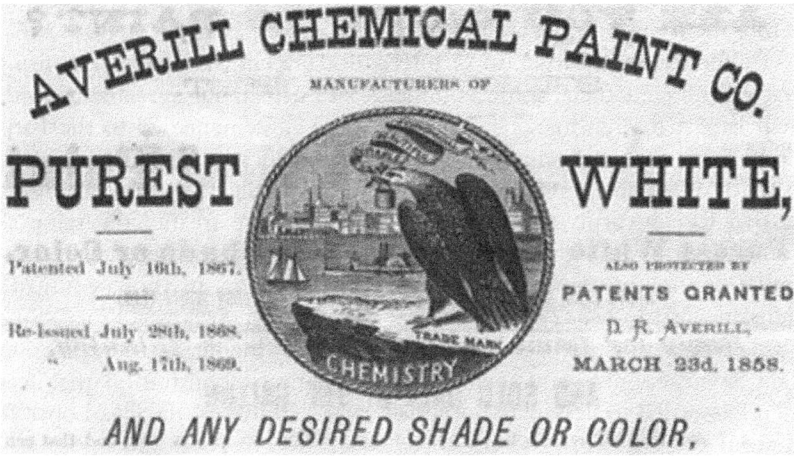

Fig. 6.1   Averill Chemic Paint Co. trademark from https://logos.fandom.com/wiki/Averill_Chemical_Paint

The new trademark statute called for federal registration of marks that had been established by use in commerce. Trademarks could only be registered in a single industry identified in the application. By the end of 1870, 121 marks were registered federally. 21 registrations were for tobacco or snuff; 10 for whisky or liquor; 9 for medicines; 6 for soaps and other cleaners; 5 for fertilizers; 4 for brooms, dry and other types of goods, and white lead; 3 for metal and metal tubing, bitters, burning fluids, various foods, and various powders. Even items like steam governors, sewing machines, wagon axles and wheels, and watches received trademarks (Commissioner of Patents, 1870, 260–261).

The industries that first adopted brand identity protection in other countries were pretty similar to those first movers in the U.S. As noted above, U.S. trademark registrations in this period covered not just pharmaceuticals and tobacco but also liquors, food, textiles, and many other products including durables like metal goods (Higgins, 2012: 266). UK tobacco firms also were some of the first to use abstract brand names starting in the 1860s (Mercer, 2010, 19).

Duguid et al. (2010) compared trademark registrations by industry in France, the US and UK. For example, in 1890, France registered about 65% trademarks for nondurable consumer products compared with 55% for the US and 43% for the UK. In 1870 and 1880, tobacco captured about 20% of registrations in the US, plummeting to 3% in 1890. In the UK, tobacco accounted for only about 5–7% of registrations during the same period with even smaller proportion of registrations in France. Medicine accounted for about 15% of US registrations in 1870–1900. France was at the same proportion in 1900 but prior to that and in the UK for the entire period medicine registrations the range was 3–8%. Beverages were the leading category of French registrations ranging from 15 to 28% but only accounted for 6%–12% of registrations in the UK and US during the same time periods. In Spain, one area, Catalonia, had almost half the trademark registrations led by textile companies and then the chemical industry and food, beverages and tobacco. The (cigarette) paper-making industry also was an early leader in trademark registrations (Saiz & Perez, 2012).

The number of marks registered annually in the U.S. quickly grew. For example, in 1876, 959 trademarks were registered across a broad range of products. Industry leaders for trademark registrations include tobacco products with 157 trademark registrations followed by liquors with 51, medical compounds and preparations with 47 and soaps with 32.

These trademark-leading industries account for only 30% of all registrations in 1876 compared to nearly 40% in 1870 (Commissioner of Patents, 1877, 427–438). Trademark registrations seem to be broadening out more industries. Branding was becoming an important marketing tool after the U.S. civil war as discussed in the next chapter.

TRADEMARK REGISTRATION SUPERSEDES DESIGN PATENT REGISTRATION

The establishment of trademark registration in 1870 led critics to argue that the practice of issuing trademarks as design patents, as described in the preceding chapter, should be abolished. Francis Upton (1860, 18–19), author of the first U.S. treatise on trademark law, criticized this practice ten years before the Trademark Act of 1870:

> It is quite obvious that such was not the purpose of the law, but, on the contrary, it was manifestly intended, that the design, for which such protection was provided –should constitute a portion of the manufactured articles, either as an ornamental adjunct, or as controlling its figure of proportions –by no means, as a mere name or designation, by which to identify or distinguish the article .... The policy of continuing such an unwarrantable construction of the law –resorted to for such a purpose [to be able to label the product as "patented" "thereby inducing the public to believe that a patent exists for the thing itself –not for the mere device or mark attached to it"] –is, to say the least, very questionable.

In a September 1870 decision appealing the denial of a patent for a trademark application, Commissioner Fisher acknowledged past practice of issuing design patents "for a trademark." He argued the latter words were merely descriptive and did not guarantee use as a trademark. In addition, any lawsuit for patent infringement would have only recovered damages for infringement of the design features but not verbal elements such as the name and labels.

Commissioner Fisher also noted that the application fee for trademark registration was cheaper ($25 instead of $30) and trademark protection at 30 years was more than double the fourteen-year term of a design patent, so why would anyone still want a design patent on a trademark? He further noted that only "forced construction" of the statute allowed the practice in the first place. The revised statute that included trademark registration made it clear that trademark protection could only be obtained by following the trademark registration provisions (Simonds, 1874, 85–87).

Thus the 1870 Patent Office report included only 22 designs designated as trademarks. The final design for a trademark patent was # 4266, dated July 26, 1870. It was for a self-sharpening hoe. True to Upton's criticism, the label design noted "H.C. Rogers, Patentee" suggesting the hoe itself was patented when in fact only the label/trademark design was patented.

THE 1870 TRADEMARK STATUTE DECLARED UNCONSTITUTIONAL

In 1876, the trademark statute was amended to add criminal penalties for fraudulent use or counterfeiting of others' marks. Three years later the 1870 trademark statute was declared unconstitutional by the U.S. Supreme Court. The 1870 statute was based on the patent and copyright clause of the Constitution. This clause (Article I, Section 8, Clause 8) authorizes Congress "To promote the progress of science and useful arts, by securing for limited times to authors and inventors the exclusive right to their respective writings and discoveries." This clause does not mention trademarks nor seek to protect marketers and their efforts to brand the products they sell. In 1879, the Supreme Court declared the Trademark Act of 1870, as amended, to be unconstitutional (*Trade-Mark Cases*, 1879). At this point some 8000 marks had been registered (Wilkins, 1992).

Despite this period of legal uncertainty, marketers continued to register trademarks. Trademark registrations quickly exceeded copyright label and print registrations from 1870 through 1905 as presented in Table 6.1.

When the Supreme Court declared the trademark registration statute unconstitutional in 1879, this also caused label applications to drop as well. However, a lower court decision the following year refused to declare the label law unconstitutional, so filings rebounded. 1883 saw a new record of filings with 834 label applications filed and 906 registrations issued (Rosen, 2012, 385).

Another federal trademark statute was adopted in 1881 but it only authorized registration for trademarks used in foreign commerce (or in commerce with Indian tribes) (Petty, 2011, 89). This led to many U.S.

Table 6.1   Print and trademark registrations by year from Petty (2012, 145)

▣ **Labels/Prints**

▣ **Trademarks**

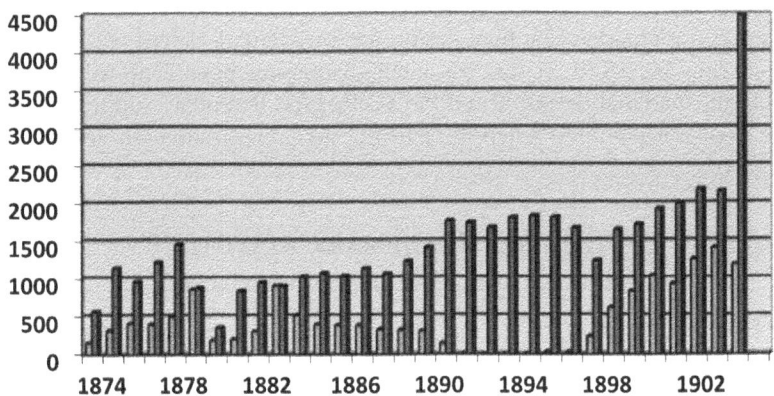

businesses making minimal international shipments just to obtain federal registration. However, in 1903, the U.S. Supreme Court held that federal courts lacked jurisdiction to enjoin infringement of a federally registered trademark unless the infringement occurred in foreign commerce (*Warner v. Searle & Hereth Co.*, 1903).

Congress reacted to the Supreme Court decision by enacting a new trademark statute in 1905 under the authority of the interstate commerce clause of the Constitution (Article 1, Section 8, Clause 3). It provided for federal registration of trademarks that had been used in interstate commerce for more than ten years. Almost 4500 trademarks were registered in 1905 (Commissioner of Patents, 1905).

U.S. Label and Print Copyright Registration Clarified

Unlike design patents of trademarks, copyright label and print registration continued, with some controversy, despite the establishment of federal trademark registration (Petty, 2012). In 1870, not only was the Patent Office authorized to register trademarks, but the Library of Congress was charged with collecting and preserving copyright documents and records. By 1872 when the number of prints, engravings, and chromos copyrights registered for the year was 4719 (over 20% of the total number of copyright registrations), the Librarian of Congress protested—arguing that commercial labels were included in these categories but were never intended to be protected by copyright laws because they did not "promote the progress of science and the useful arts" as required by the Constitution.

He recommended instead that they be registered in the Patent Office as either trademarks or designs of labels. He admitted that it had "always been customary to enter for copyright large numbers of printed labels, with or without pictorial embellishment, designed for use on cigarboxes, patent medicines, and other articles of manufacturer" (Librarian of Congress, 1872, 4–5).

In response, Congress enacted a confusing law in 1874 that stated commercial prints and labels could not be registered under the copyright laws at the Library of Congress but could be registered by the Patent Office. The statute also said that labels and prints registered in the Patent Office could not be trademarks, although the trademark department would handle label/print applications. In 1881, the Commissioner of Patents decided that the word "prints" in the statute meant printer labels, nothing more. It was not until 1893 that "prints" were recognized as a separate category from labels encompassing printed advertisements. Applications for label registrations substantially exceeded print applications through 1930 when the Office stopped reporting on these two categories separately (Rosen, 2012, 335–356, 385–387).

Attempts to register labels with the Library of Congress continued for another twenty years, but such applications were usually forwarded to the Patent Office (Rosen, 2012, 356; 2023, 501). The change in registration location for commercial prints and labels caused the numbers of prints registered in the copyright office to drop from 5598 in 1874 to 1639 in 1875. This drop in registrations of almost 4000 between 1874 and 1875, the Patent Office did not see a corresponding increase in label (including print) registrations. Just over 400 labels were registered annually between 1876 and 1879 (Rosen, 2012, 356). While the number of label registrations was significant during this time, often twice as many trademarks were registered. Perhaps marketers were struggling with the

changing copyright rules, and some switched relying on trademark registration instead of copyright registration for the entire label or poster
advertisement.

The number of labels registered by the Patent Office probably does
not reflect the total number of labels for which copyright protection was
sought. Labels were still being submitted to federal district courts. The
US District Court for the District of Massachusetts registered 33 labels
and trademarks between 1874 and 1878. Most of the entries in the record
book include a copy of the actual label or trademark (Record for Applications for Labels and Trade Marks from 1874 to 1878 is available at
the US National Archives ARC Identifier 2945743). It is not clear what
proportion of these labels and trademarks were also registered with the
Patent Office.

The meaning and implications of the language of the new 1874 statute
were debated for years. For example, the statute did not define labels or
prints. Initially both were registered in a single category, but the Commissioner of Patents believed prints were pressed onto articles of manufacture
whereas labels were slips of paper attached to articles of manufacture. In
1881, the Commissioner changed his position and asserted that prints
were simply printed labels (Rosen, 2012, 355–356).

The Patent Office also refused to treat label registration as a ministerial copyright registration that was automatically registered. Rather, the
Patent Office examined labels and prints for appropriateness of registration, just as they did for patents and trademarks. Indeed, the Patent
Office's 1885 rules described the prior practice of the Librarian of
Congress to register commercial prints and labels as copyrights as merely
providing a "semblance of protection to many trade-marks, of which the
labels and prints entered by him were the mere vehicles" (Rosen, 2012,
360). Thus, the Librarian of Congress believed that trademark protection
should be the primary goal of marketers rather than seeking to protect
the entire label.

CASE STUDY: SAMSON ROPE
TRADEMARK REGISTRATION STRATEGY

Samson Rope has the distinction of the oldest U.S. registered trademark
(1884) that is still in use today (Figs. 6.2 and 6.3).

The company was founded by J. P. Tolman in 1878 after grad-
uating from the Massachusetts Institute of Technology that year. In

Int. Cl.: 22

Prior U.S. Cl.: 7

United States Patent and Trademark Office
10 Year Renewal

Reg. No. 11,210
Registered May 27, 1884
Renewal Term Begins May 27, 1994

TRADEMARK
PRINCIPAL REGISTER

SAMSON

SAMSON OCEAN SYSTEMS, INC. (DELAWARE CORPORATION) 2090 THORNTON STREET FERNDALE, WA 98248, BY ASSIGNMENT, CHANGE OF NAME AND ASSIGNMENT FROM TOLMAN, JAMPES P. (UNITED STATES CITIZEN) BOSTON, MA

SUCH FACSIMILE REPRESENTS PICTORIALLY THE SCRIPTURAL CHARACTER SAMSON IN THE ACT OF SLAYING A LION.

FOR: CORDS, LINES, [TWINES,] AND ROPES, IN CLASS 7 (INT. CL. 22).

FIRST USE 1-1-1884; IN COMMERCE 1-1-1884.

SER. NO. 70-011,210, FILED 4-7-1884.

Fig. 6.2   1884 trademark

1883, Tolman received his first patent in Canada (No. CA17513A) for a "Machine for making cordage, webbing, etc." The company obtained over thirty additional patents between 1896 and 1963 and became known as an innovator. In 1888, Tolman incorporated Samson Cordage Works in Massachusetts and began producing the first braided rope with a reinforced core (Fig. 6.4).

Fig. 6.3 Trademark Promoting its Oldest Registration from https://logos.fan dom.com/wiki/Samson_Rope

Fig. 6.4 From The Inland Architect & News Record (August 1888)

It also sought to protect its reputation as an innovative brand by actively pursuing trademark protection. First, since it did not always use its 1884 trademark in the same form of its registration, in 1906, it registered the word "Samson" (U.S. Reg. 50828) and the picture of Samson battling the lion without the company name or any other words (U.S. Reg. 51775). Both trademarks are still in effect today. In 2008, it registered "The Strongest Name in Rope" (U.S. Reg. 3364731). It disclaimed any possible protection of just the word rope using this word trademark. It has used this word mark in addition to its 1884 and 1906 marks.

Second, Samson's 1888 braided rope with a reinforced core was produced with periodic spots braided into its design. In 1893, the

Fig. 6.5 From *American Carpenter & Builder* (August 1906)

company registered a picture trademark of the words Spot Cord in a rectangle (U.S. Reg No. 23509). Fifteen years later, it registered a word mark for Spot Cord (U.S. Reg. No. 23509) in 1908. The word mark is in effect and still being used today. The company may have thought the words themselves were merely descriptive of the cord's appearance, so it waited until the name came to indicate the origin of the goods to most consumers and then registered the words themselves (Fig. 6.5).

Following its initial trademark success, Samson developed some twenty additional trademarks that were often suggestive. For example, Fig. 6.6 is a 1957 advertisement for Tite Rope suggesting its use for a taut clothesline. It also mentions Spot Cord and shows eight other products that are difficult to read.

Registered trademarks provide notice to competitors of what marks they should not imitate. However, if a rival closely imitates a mark, the registrant should be prepared to sue to enforce its exclusive rights. In 1924, Samson obtained an injunction against a Melbourne Australia cord firm that advertised "Samson Cordage," "Lion Cordage," "Samson Brand," and "Lion Brand." The Australian company also sold "Dot Cord"—a rope with a different color of thread braided into the rope to produce a dot pattern. The similarities between spot and dot and the rope itself were compelling The Australian court enjoined all of these practices as violative of Samson's trademarks (Cordage Trade Marks, 1924).

Despite its registration of its portfolio of trademarks, Samson Rope was caught unprepared for acquiring a domain name. Samson.com was

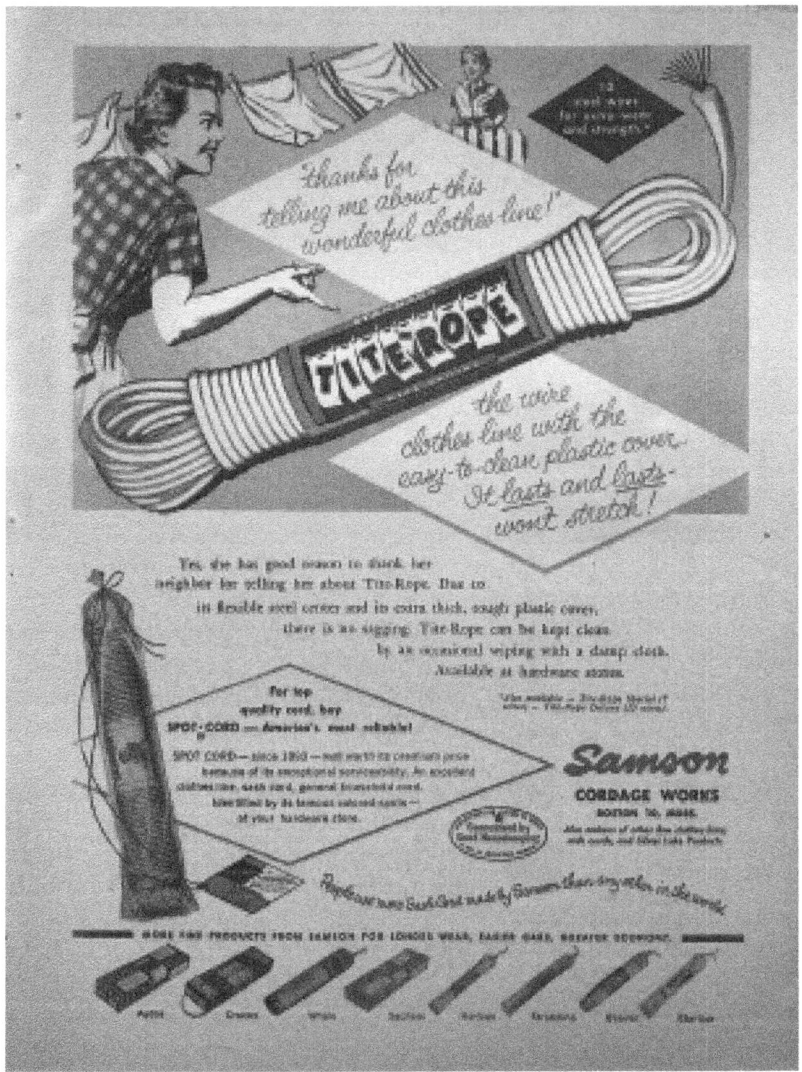

Fig. 6.6 From the Samson Timeline (2024)

taken by an oil drilling company in 1994. To be fair, many other firms containing the word Samson would have been interested in that domain name. Sampson Rope acquired samsonrope.com in 2000 (DomainGang, 2020).

References

Bleistein v. Donaldson Lithographing Co. (1903), 188 U.S. 239.

Commissioner of Patents. (Various Years). *Annual Report of the Commissioner of Patents*. Government Printing Office.

Cordage Trade Marks. (1924, September 11). *The Age*, 24.

Derringer v. Plate (1865), 29 Cal. 292 (California Supreme Court).

DomainGang. (2020, February 21). *#Samson: Oldest Live #Trademark at the #USPTO Comes Without the Matching .com #Domain Name*. Retrieved July 10, 2024, from https://domaingang.com/domain-news/samson-oldest-live-trademark-at-the-uspto-comes-without-the-matching-com-domain-name/

Duguid, P. (2009). French Connections: The International Propagation of Trademarks in the Nineteenth Century. *Enterprise & Society, 10*(1), 3–37.

Duguild, P. (2013). California Marketing & Collective Amnesia. *University of California Davis Law Review, 47*(2), 581–600.

Duguid, P., da Silva Lopes, T., & Mercer, J. (2010). Reading Registrations: An Overview of 100 Years of Trademark Registrations in France, the United Kingdom and the United States. In T. da Silva Lopes & P. Duguid (Eds.), *Trademarks, Brands, and Competitiveness* (pp. 9–30). Routledge.

Higgins v. Keuffel (1891), 140 U.S. 428.

Higgins, D. M. (2008). The Making of Modern Trade Mark Law: The UK, 1860–1914, A Business History Perspective. In L. Bently, J. Davis, & J. C. Ginsburg (Eds.), *Trademarks and Brands: An Interdisciplinary Critique* (pp. 42–61). Cambridge University Press.

Higgins, D. M. (2012). Forgotten Heroes and Forgotten Issues: Business and Trademark History during the Nineteenth Century. *Business History Review, 86*(2), 261–285.

Librarian of Congress. (1872), *Annual Report of the Librarian of Congress*. Government Printing Office.

Mercer, J. (2010). A mark of distinction: Branding and trade mark law in the UK from the 1860s. *Business History, 52*(1), 17–42.

Petty, R. D. (2011). Labels and Trademarks and Prints, Oh My! Legal Evidence of US Interest in Brand Protection in the 1800s. In L. Neilson (Ed.), *Marketing History in the New World, Proceedings of the 15th Biennial Conference in Historical Analysis & Research in Marketing (CHARM)* (pp. 145–156).

Petty, R. D. (2012). From Label to Trademark: The Legal Origins of the Concept of Brand Identity in Nineteenth Century America. *Journal of Historical Research in Marketing, 4*(1), 129–153.

Rosen, Z. S. (2009). In Search of the Trademark Cases: The Nascent Treaty Power and the Turbulent Origins of Federal Trademark Law. *St. John's Law Review, 83*(Summer), 827–904.

Rosen, Z. S. (2012). Reimagining Bleistein: Copyright for Advertisements in Historical Perspective. *Journal of the Copyright Society U.S.A., 59*(Winter), 347–389. Retrieved from SSRN: https://ssrn.com/abstract=1507125 or https://doi.org/10.2139/ssrn.1507125

Rosen, Z. S. (2023). Examining Copyright. *Journal of the Copyright Society of the USA, 69,* 481–564. Retrieved from SSRN: https://ssrn.com/abstract=4099976 or https://doi.org/10.2139/ssrn.4099976

The Samson Timeline. (2024). Retrieved July 10, 2024, from https://www.samsonrope.com/about/timeline#:~:text=%E2%80%8B1884%3A%20The%20company's%20now,1889%3A%20American%20Manufacturing%20Co

Saiz, P., & Perez, P. F. (2012). Catalonian Trademarks and the Development of Marketing Knowledge in Spain, 1850–1946. *Business History Review, 86*(2), 239–260.

da Silva Lopes, T., & Casson, M. (2012). Imitation, Brand Protection and Globalization of British Business. *Business History Review, 86*(2), 287–310.

Simonds, W. E. (1874). *The Law of Design Patents.* Baker Voorhis & Co.

Trade-Mark Cases (1879), 100 U.S. 82.

United States Congress. (1900). *Report of the Commissioners Appointed to Revise the Statutes Relating to Patents, Trade and Other Marks, and Trade and Commercial Names.* Government Printing Office.

Upton, F. H. (1860). *A Treatise on the Law of Trade Marks.* Little Law Bookseller.

Warner v. Searle & Hereth Co. (1903), 191 U.S. 195.

Wilkins, M. (1992). The Neglected Intangible Asset: The Influence of the Trade Mark on the Rise of the Modern Corporation. *Business History, 34*(1), 66–95.

CHAPTER 7

Turn-of-the-Century Brand Marketing and Legal Protection

Abstract The late 1800s saw increased trademark protection, particularly for marks that were distinctive rather than descriptive. Technical trademarks were distinguished from trade names. The latter were enforced by "passing off" lawsuits under unfair competition rather than trademark infringement. Copyright protection of labels was clarified and the U.S. Supreme Court also definitively ruled that copyright law protects artistic images and expression used in advertising. This would encourage brand image advertising.

Keywords Technical trademarks · Trade names · Passing off · Advertising · Brand image · Patent medicines · Nostrums

INTRODUCTION

The latter half of the nineteenth century, particularly in the U.S., is generally recognized as the period when brand marketing, enabled by the development of trademark law, took off. While certain industries such as medicines, tobacco, and alcohol took the lead in brand marketing, by the turn-of-the-century, the practice appears widespread. Business historians

© The Author(s), under exclusive license to Springer Nature Switzerland AG 2024
R. D. Petty, *From Marking Products to Marketing Brands*, Palgrave Studies in Marketing, Organizations and Society,
https://doi.org/10.1007/978-3-031-76778-4_7

attribute the rise in trademark use and modern branding to industrialization during the latter 1800s. Jones (1986) suggests that brands evolved as further protection for new inventions that were covered by utility patents but only for a limited time. Patented processes that improved the consistency and quality of manufactured items needed brands to assure consumers that they could consistently identify these high-quality items.

Strasser (1989) generally agrees with this analysis but adds that patented products and methods of factory production were aided in the development of modern national brands by national consumer product distribution systems such as parcel post in 1912, color printing techniques, and the development of the "new media"—magazines that allowed brands to relate to particular lifestyles and personalities. Furthermore, the country was becoming increasingly urban and urban factory workers purchased more goods rather than self-produce them as farmers tended to do (Tedlow, 1990). This led to additional demands for brand identity protection and is a watershed period for brand identity protection if not brand centric marketing.

However as noted in Chapter 6, marketers continued to face questions about whether creative expression (words or images) used on labels or in advertising could be registered for copyright protection and presumed to be protectable from unauthorized copying. Courts and policymakers also had to decide which words and other devices could be protected under trademark law. In addition, the 1881 federal trademark act re-established federal registration but only for marks used in foreign commerce. Marks used only domestically would not be registrable again until the 1905 act. The turn-of-the-century would see several improvements in both trademark and copyright law that would benefit developing brand marketers.

The U.S. Supreme Court Considers Labels and Prints

From 1885 through 1890, Patent Office label registrations (including prints at that time) declined from about 400–300 annually (Rosen, 2012). Trademark registrations, in contrast, increased from twice to four times the number of label registrations. Label registrations dropped to zero after an 1891 Supreme Court decision that denied registration to a simple label containing three words in ordinary type: "Waterproof Drawing Ink." Clearly, Charles M. Higgins, who marketed the ink, had no sense of branding the product as coming from a particular company or even himself much less promoting the company name or any brand name. The Court noted that the plaintiff was not asserting trademark rights to the label and this label did not function like a trademark, i.e., distinguishing goods from one seller from those of other sellers (*Higgins v. Keuffel*, 1891, 433).

The Court held that registering such a descriptive label did not advance science or the useful arts and therefore was not authorized under the patent and copyright provision of the U.S. Constitution. It also held that copyrighted works must exhibit some originality and be "founded in the creative powers of the mind" (*Higgins v. Keuffel*, 1891, 431; Zimmerman, 2006, 89). The year after *Higgins* only six labels were registered. The following three years there were none (Rosen, 2012, 364).

The Patent Office quickly responded to this decision by holding in 1892 that commercial labels that were sufficiently artistic could be registered. The following year in a case involving Heinz, the well-known condiments brand, the Commissioner of Patents recognized for the first time that prints were a separate category under the 1874 statute. Prints must be registered as such, not as labels. However, also in 1893, the Office issued a rule denying label registration for labels that contained a trademark. Five years later in 1898, the Office discarded its rule and held that prints could contain trademarks and still be registered and that trademarks could even appear on labels if they were not the totality of the label (Rosen, 2012, 365–366).

The Patent Office's now expansive interpretation of the 1874 statute was soon supported by the Supreme Court. In a case involving three circus advertising posters, presented below, Justice Holmes held in his majority opinion that "A picture is none the less a subject of copyright that it is used for an advertisement" (*Bleistein v. Donaldson Lithographing Co.*, 1903, 431). This support for copyrights on commercial labels and prints led to a new high of registrations totaling 1732 in 1904 and a peak of 1365 in 1906 (Rosen, 2012, 385) (Fig. 7.1).

By 1940, the 1874 Act was repealed and copyrights of pictures, whether of fine art or commercial prints or labels, were again administered by the Copyright Office in the Library of Congress (Rosen, 2012, 382). Original and artistic labels and advertisements continue to receive copyright protection today.

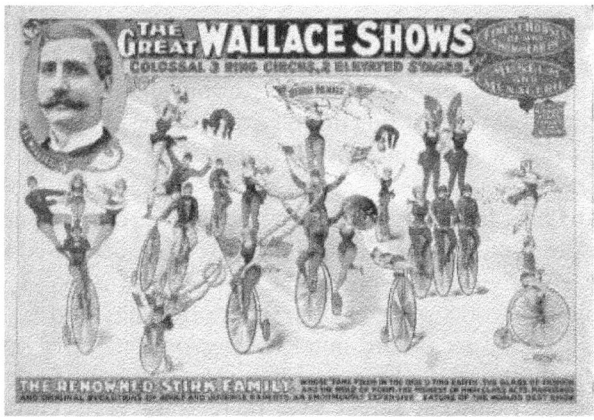

Fig. 7.1 Wallace Shows Advertising Posters from https://parkerhiggins.net/2015/01/3-circus-posters-changed-face-copyright-law/

BRAND IMAGE PROMOTION

Trademark and copyright law evolved separately to increase protection from imitators for both trademarks and copyright-protected images. Color lithography enabled large colorful advertising posters in the post-Civil War U.S. as illustrated above and in the Chapter 5 discussion of trade cards. Posters became quite popular in the latter 1800s. Posters typically featured the name of advertised brand and an image that the marketer sought to associate with the brand (Richards, 2022, 144). Thus, protecting advertising posters and labels themselves from imitation would encourage so-called image advertising of branded products to establish a platform for developing relationships with consumers (Dawar, 2004).

One form of image advertising was the use of works of art from established artists. Pears Soap purchased the image of a boy playing with bubbles that it used that in 1887 to start a campaign of image advertising with many color images and some racist in both wording and image (Richards, 2022, 122–123). Bicycle advertising posters also used artwork from famous artists on occasion, but the industry was more well known for using images related to product performance such as flight, speed, lightness of weight, and ease of pedaling (Petty, 1995) (Figs. 7.2 and 7.3).

Another common form of image advertising was the use of a character, either real (e.g., the Smith Brothers who sold cough drops) or made-up (e.g., biblical strongman Samson who sold rope). While image and character trademarks were quite popular in the mid-twentieth century, their

Fig. 7.2 Pears Soap advertising poster

Fig. 7.3 Bicycle
advertising posters

use started with turn-of-the century people and characters. One of the earliest was *La Belle Chocolatiere* by the Swiss artist Jean-étienne Liotard. The right to use this image in advertising was obtained by the Baker's Chocolate Company in 1836 (other sources say 1862). While this is a portrait of a real person, it also qualifies as fine art from a known artist. Over fifty years later (1877) the Quaker Oats Man was the first trademark for a breakfast cereal. Lydia E. Pinkham introduced her Vegetable Compound in 1875. She agreed to put her portrait on package in 1879 thereby increasing sales (Cross, 2002, 17–19). Aunt Jamima was created in 1893 using the image of product demonstrator Nancy Green. One final example is the Michelin Man (Cross, 2002, 31–34)—a character made up in 1898 to "swallow the bumps in the road" (Richards, 2022, 288). These characters represented their brands by presenting a specific human (or human-like) image to appeal to consumers (Fig. 7.4).

The Scope of Trademark Protection

Although trademark registrations in the U.S. consistently exceeded label and print registrations at this time, there were still questions about what sorts of names, words, signs, and other devices could be protected as trademarks (Higgins, 2012, 271–274). In Britain, the 1862 Merchandise Mark Act defined trademark to include words and names but only provided for criminal sanctions for intentional use of another's mark to defraud (Bently, 2008, 9–10). The 1875 Trademark Act was the first in Britain to provide for registration of trademarks but permitted registration of individual or firm names only if they were presented in a distinctive manner, such as an individual's signature. This act reversed the broad definition in the 1862 act, by excluding mere words even if they were invented or fanciful in the industry context or were otherwise non-descriptive of the products they identified.

Like U.S. courts, British courts struggled to determine which words in the context of a specific industry were too descriptive to merit protecting them as a trademark belonging to only one firm (Bently, 2008, 22–23, 27). British courts also struggled with geographic marks that indicated the place of manufacture since its guild history was based on geography (Bently, 2008, 26, 30–31). The concepts of "fancy words" and later "invented words" appeared on the debate in the latter 1800s. The precise definition of these concepts eluded the legal system until the UK 1905 Trademark Act clarified that only words making direct reference to the

Fig. 7.4 The
Chocolate Girl (1836/
1862), The Quaker Oats
Man (1877), Lydia E.
Pinkham (1879), Aunt
Jamina (1893), and the
Michelin Man (1898)
from left to right

Fig. 7.4 (continued)

quality or character of the goods could not be registered (Mercer, 2010, 25).

In contrast, in 1824 France expanded its law to protect names and places of manufacturers from imitation (Duguid et al., 2010, 24). Similarly, the Germanic countries of Germany, Austria, and the Netherlands excluded words commonly used in an industry as well as marks consisting or mere letters, words, or numbers or the arms of states or countries. Soon after Denmark, Switzerland, the Netherlands, Germany, Sweden, and Japan all allowed word trademarks that were not descriptive. Switzerland set up separate protection for geographic indicators (Bently, 2008,

40). In 1905, Britain also allowed geographic indicators to be registered as certification marks (Higgins, 2008, 60).

U.S. TECHNICAL TRADEMARKS

The U.S. experienced similar discussions about what words and other signs should be treated as trademarks and which should not. By the late 1800s in the U.S., protectable trademarks became known as technical trademarks (Barrett, 2008, 903–904). As the court explained in Davis v. Davis (1886, 491–492), "A trade-mark is some arbitrary or representative device attached to or sold with merchandise and serving to designate the origin or manufacture of that merchandise." Trademarks were registrable under the 1905 Act and protected from trademark infringement by focusing on the similarity of the imitation mark with that of the original mark when used on products in the same industry. A number of court cases found infringement for use in similar but not identical industries such as axes and shovels, automobiles and tires, and baking powder and baking soda (Lukens, 1927, 200).

For technical trademarks, the complaining party did not need to prove the imitator's intent and whether consumers were diverted from purchasing the brand they intended to buy (McKenna, 2007). As the Supreme Court noted: "If a plaintiff has the absolute right to the use of a particular word or words as a trade-mark, then, if an infringement is shown, the wrongful or fraudulent intent is presumed..." (*Elgin National Watch Co. v. Illinois Watch Case Co.*, 1901, 674). The Supreme Court also recognized that technical trademarks were a form of property based on use in commerce (*Trade-Mark Cases*, 1879). This theory was consistent with the natural rights theory of law that was popular at the time and courts sought to grant property rights to those who created property through their own efforts (McKenna, 2007).

In contrast to technical trademarks that could be registered under the 1905 act, trade names identified the source of products but did so with descriptive (e.g., company founder or location) names. Such terms should be available to competitors to use honestly which is the beginning of the modern concept of trademark fair use. Therefore, such descriptive names could not be registered under the 1905 Act unless used exclusively in commerce for ten years prior to the enactment of the act.

Such names were only protected when intentional imitation by competitors caused consumers to be confused about product source

(Bone, 2006, 564–566; Lane, 1909). Such lawsuits (often called passing off rather than trademark infringement) were based on fraud and typically required proof of the intent of the second user to confuse consumers (*Amoskeag Mfg. Co. v. Spear*, 1837; *Lawrence Mfg. Co. v. Tennessee Mfg. Co.*, 1891). Remedies were typically limited. While technical trademark infringements typically were remedied with a complete injunction, trade name imitation was only enjoined if the imitator failed to clearly identify the source of the product and distinguish it from the first user (Handler & Pickett, 1930).

Room (1998) examined brand names of leading American advertisers in the 1890s and developed the following categories that can be divided into trade names and technical trademarks. Trade names include Room's categories of personal names, place names, and descriptive names (e.g., Shredded Wheat or 57 for Heinz's variety of products). In contrast, Room's categories of good association names (e.g., Sunlight soap), status names (e.g., Monarch bicycles), invented scientific names (e.g., Cuticura Soap), and artificial names (e.g., Kodak) all appear to qualify for technical trademark registration and protection. While Room treats all place names as descriptive, arbitrary place names could be registered if they had proven secondary meaning, e.g., Vienna bread (*Fleischman v. Shuckmann*, 1881). Secondary meaning had developed as a judicial concept that would allow brand marketers to earn the right through extensive advertising and promotion of exclusive use of a particular descriptive name in the sale of their type of goods. As noted above, this right was limited allowing rivals to use that same description so long as consumers were not confused about the source of the other products (Lane, 1909).

Once registered federally, trademarks were presumed valid throughout the country, so the courts no longer allowed innocent second users in local geographic markets to use the same trademarked name. This change recognized the growing importance of national brands and brands that wanted to be national in scope. Instead of lasting only 30 years, trademarks would now last 20 years but could be renewed indefinitely (Petty, 2011).

Strasser (1989, 45) states that pent up demand for domestic mark registration led to over 10,000 applications for trademark registrations to be filed during the first year of the 1905 Act. It also seems likely that many of these applicants also realized that this would be the only time that descriptive trade names in use for more than ten years could be registered as trademarks. The new law also eliminated intent to prove infringement, but infringement was limited to use of an identical or confusingly similar mark on "merchandise of the same descriptive qualities" as those for which the original mark was registered.

The legal development of technical trademark protection as distinct from, and more easily proven than, passing off is important for the history of brand marketing because it encouraged businesses to switch from the traditional practice of identifying products solely by company name. Companies often took the name of their location or the personal name(s) of the company founder(s). Since other companies in the same location or with founders of the same name also were entitled to use such trade names, brands marketed under such names were less likely to be distinctly identified in the minds of consumers. The development and use of technical trademarks allowed brand marketing to focus on abstract rather than descriptive brand identifiers.

However, at the same time, courts began to develop the concept of secondary meaning. Secondary meaning occurs when consumers recognize that a descriptive trade name identifies a particular brand rather than merely describing goods. Once, a plaintiff proved its mark had secondary meaning, courts treated such marks like technical trademarks with less focus on the intent of the imitator and broader remedies (Lane, 1909).

Some devices that are available for current trademark protection were not protected at the turn-of-the-century. Slogans could not be registered because they were considered advertisements rather than trademarks that had to be affixed to the product. Similarly, products themselves, packages, and particular colors were not considered trademarks because they were not marks affixed to products (Thompson, 1911). The affixation requirement was another enabler of the modern concept of fair use. For example, advertising terms that were not otherwise affixed to the product were not legally protected and were available for others to copy (Barrett, 2010).

Unfortunately, it is difficult to tell the extent to which trademarks were promoted to create a brand identity. Some of the symbols were clearly descriptive showing the product in use (Petty, 2012, 134). Others may have been simple stock woodcut images to attract visual appeal. Still others, like patent medicines, often used symbols of re-assurance such as angels, doctors, and grandmothers, symbols of power or symbols of exotic origin (Laird, 1998, 16–18). Perhaps those symbols helped define a brand identity in some cases.

CASE STUDY: PATENT MEDICINES

Perhaps the most well-known examples of the English government providing an exclusive right "patent" to particular companies are so-called patent medicines. Although most such nostrums did not obtain a utility patent, the name of patent medicines was applied to the entire nostrum industry. Even though often criticized as frauds, nostrums were among the earliest industries in the development of brand identification, brand packaging, and ultimately brand marketing. The period from the American Civil War to the passage of the 1906 U.S. Pure Food and Drugs Act was the golden age of American patent medicines (Young, 1961).

The U.S. Patent Office granted 86 utility patents for medicines by 1849 (Billings, 1892). Most other medicines that registered with the Patent Office did so for other purposes. Their bottles or labels were registered as design patents or copyright-protected as labels. In fact, patent medicines were the second largest industry registrants of trademark design patents with 32 between 1855 and 1870, exceeded only by the personal care and clothing industry with 42. For trademarks registered during the first year of federal registration (1870), tobacco led with 21 registrations followed by liquor and medicines (Petty, 2012).

Branded nostrums were promoted for their purportedly unique ability to treat numerous maladies cheaply and quickly (compared to doctors who were perceived as expensive and extensive in the duration of treatment) (Laird, 1998; Young, 1961, 169). The popular nostrums were mass produced in laboratory/factories and distributed nationwide and even globally rather than concocted on demand by a pharmacist or physician.

Nostrum sellers were among the first to appreciate the marketing importance of a well-known trademark in both promoting a new product and differentiating it from other similar products (Laird, 1998). Norris (1990) estimates that patent medicines placed more newspaper and magazine ads in the latter 1800s than any other industry category. Some estimate that by the 1870s, 25% of all advertising was for propriety drugs (Anderson, 2000). Others estimate that by 1870, nostrum ads accounted for half of all advertisements (Goodrum & Dalrymple, 1990; Laird, 1998).

More than half of the "top advertiser" firms listed in 1893 as spending $50,000 or more annually on national advertising were proprietary medicine firms (Laird, 1998). An 1898 survey of 2,853 national or regional advertisers found that nearly 15% sold medicines (Pope, 1983).

Even as national brands developed in other industries such as Royal Baking Powder, Sapolio, Pear's Soap, and Ivory Soap, they were still out-advertised in the 1880s and 1890s by the top patent medicine brands (Laird, 1998). By the early twentieth century, patent medicines placed an estimated $40 million per year of advertising (Stage, 1979).

With the large amount of advertising by nostrums, it is not surprising that they played an important role in the development of the modern advertising industry generally. Laird (1998) notes that the nostrum industry was particularly important to members of the nascent advertising industry by providing experience in writing advertising copy. Wood (1958) states that most advertising agents of the 1890s had not only started in the patent medicine industry but even at that date, patent medicines remained their largest accounts. These agencies included arguably the oldest in the U.S., N.W. Ayer & Son that started in 1868 and soon worked with multiple proprietary medicines. In 1877–78, over 20% of Ayer's advertising placements were for patent medicines (Laird, 1998). Later, Claude C. Hopkins, who first formulated the concept of "reason why" advertising, would pitch various nostrums using this technique throughout his career (Wood, 1958).

This industry was important not only because of its sales revenue and advertising expenditure, but because it was one of the first to sell consumer-sized packages of uniquely branded products advertised to consumers as opposed to bulk goods sold generically to wholesalers and retailers. They also often offered medical advice booklets/almanacs and other items as product promotions (Strasser, 1989, 164–165). Tobacco companies soon followed this formula to sell their brands (Sivulka, 1998, 48). Marketers in other industries followed these two leaders in brand marketing (Fig. 7.5).

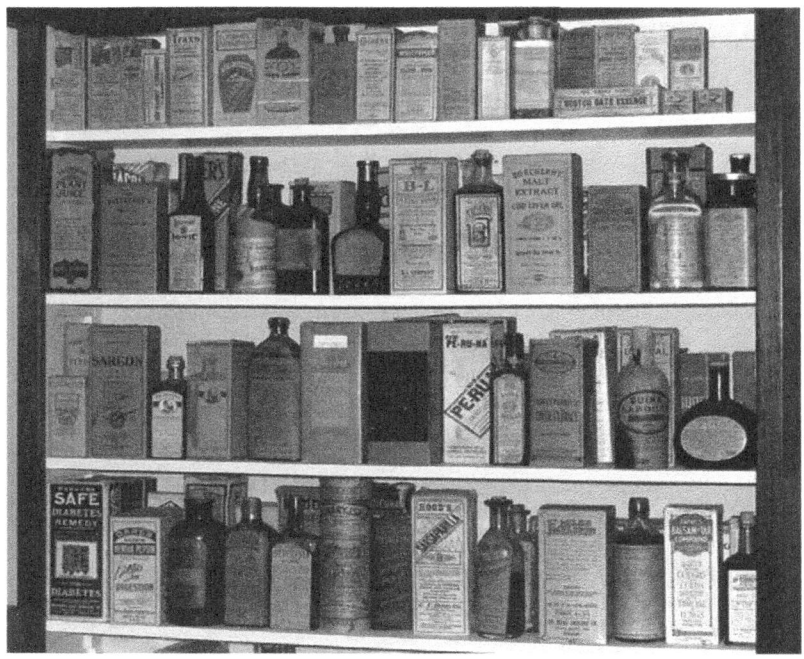

Fig. 7.5 Patent Medicines from Petty (2011, 88)

REFERENCES

Amoskeag Mfg. Co. v. Spear. (1837). 2 Sand. 599 (N.Y. Sup. Ct.).

Anderson, A. (2000). *Snake Oil, Hustlers, and Hambones: The American Medical Show*. McFarland and Co.

Barrett, M. (2008). Finding Trademark Use: The Historical Foundation for Limiting Infringement Liability to Uses "in the Manner of a Mark." *Wake Forest Law Review, 43*(Winter), 893–977.

Barrett, M. (2010). Reconciling Fair Use and Trademark Use. *Cardozo Arts & Entertainment Law Journal, 28*(1), 1–63.

Bently, L. (2008). The Making of Modern Trade Mark Law: The Construction of the Legal Concept of Trademark. In L. Bently, J. Davis, & J. C. Ginsburg (Eds.), *Trademarks and Brands: An Interdisciplinary Critique* (pp. 3–14). Cambridge University Press.

Billings, J. S. (1892). American Invention and Discoveries in Medicine, Surgery, and Practical Sanitation. In *Celebration of the Beginning of the Second Century of the American Patent System* (pp. 413–422). Government Printing Office.

Bleistein v. Donaldson Lithographing Co. (1903). 188 U.S. 239.

Bone, R. G. (2006, June). Hunting Goodwill: A History of the Concept of Goodwill in Trademark Law. *Boston University Law Review, 86,* 547–622.

Cross, M. (2002). *A Century of American Icons.* Greenwood Press.

Davis v. Davis (1886). 27 F. 490 (C.C.D. Mass.).

Dawar, N. (2004). What Are Brands Good For? *MIT Sloan Management Review, 46*(1), 31–37.

Duguid, P., da Silva Lopes, T., & Mercer, J. (2010). Reading Registrations: An Overview of 100 Years of Trademark Registrations in France, the United Kingdom and the United States. In T. da Silva Lopes & P. Duguid (Eds.), *Trademarks, Brands, and Competitiveness* (pp. 9–30). Routledge.

Elgin National Watch Co. v. Illinois Watch Case Co. (1901) 179 U.S. 665.

Goodrum, C., & Dalrymple, H. (1990). *Advertising in America: The First 200 Years.* Abrams Inc.

Higgins v. Keuffel (1891) 140 U.S. 428.

Higgins, D. M. (2008). The making of modern trade mark law: the UK, 1860-1914, A business history perspective. in Bently, L., Davis J. and Ginsburg J.C. (Eds.), *Trademarks and Brands: An Interdisciplinary Critique* (pp. 42–61). Cambridge University Press.

Higgins, D. M. (2012). Forgotten Heroes and Forgotten Issues: Business and Trademark History During the Nineteenth Century. *Business History Review, 86*(2), 261–285.

Jones, J. P. (1986). *What's in a Name?: Advertising and the Concept of Brands.* Lexington Books.

Laird, P. W. (1998). *Advertising Progress: American Business and the Rise of Consumer Marketing.* The John Hopkins University Press.

Lane, W. R. (1909). Development of Secondary Rights in Trade Mark Cases. *Yale Law Journal, 18*(8), 571–582.

Lawrence Mfg. Co. v. Tennessee Mfg. Co. (1891). 138 U.S. 537.

Lukens, E. C. (1927). The Application of the Principles of Unfair Competition in Cases of Dissimilar Products. *University of Pennsylvania Law Review and American Law Register, 75*(3), 197–206.

McKenna, M. (2007). The Normative Foundations of Trademark Law. *Notre Dame Law Review, 82*(5), 1839–1916.

Mercer, J. (2010). A Mark of Distinction: Branding and Trade Mark Law in the UK from the 1860s. *Business History, 52*(1), 17–42.

Milton Handler, M., & Pickett, C. (1930). Trade-Marks and Trade Names—An Analysis and Synthesis. *Columbia Law Review, 30*(6), 168–201.

National Biscuit Co. v. Baker. (1899). 95 F. 135.

Norris, J. D. (1990). *Advertising and the Transformation of American Society, 1865–1920.* Greenwood Press.

Petty, R. D. (1995). Peddling the Bicycle in the 1890s: Mass Marketing Shifts into High Gear. *Journal of Macromarketing, 15*(1), 32–46.

Petty, R. D. (2011). The Codevelopment of Trademark Law and the Concept of Brand Marketing in the United States Before 1946. *Journal of Macromarketing, 31*(1), 85–100.

Petty, R. D. (2012). From label to trademark: The legal origins of the concept of brand identity in nineteenth century America. *Journal of Historical Research in Marketing, 4*(1), 129–153.

Pope, D. (1983). *The Making of Modern Advertising*. Basic Books.

Richards, J. I. (2022). *A History of Advertising: The First 300,000 Years*. Bowman & Littlefield.

Room, A. (1998). The History of Branding. In S. Hart & J. Murphy (Eds.), *Brands: The New Wealth Creators* (pp. 13–23). New York University Press.

Rosen, Z. S. (2012). Reimagining Bleistein: Copyright for Advertisements in Historical Perspective. *Journal of the Copyright Society U.S.A., 59*(Winter), 347–389, from SSRN: https://ssrn.com/abstract=1507125 or https://doi.org/10.2139/ssrn.1507125

Sivulka, J. (1998). *Soap, Sex, and Cigarettes: A Cultural History of Advertising*. Wadsworth Publishing Co.

Stage, S. (1979). *Female Complaints: Lydia Pinkham and the Business of Women's Medicine*. W.W. Norton & Co.

Strasser, S. (1989). *Satisfaction Guaranteed: The Making of the American Mass Market*. Pantheon Books.

Tedlow, R. S. (1990). *New and Improved: The Story of Mass Marketing in America*. Basic Books.

Thompson, J. W. Co. (1911). *Things to Know About Trade-Marks: A Manual of Trade-Mark Information*. J. Walter Thompson Co.

Trade-Mark Cases (1879), 100 U.S. 82.

Wood, J. P. (1958). *The Story of Advertising*. The Ronald Press Co.

Young, J. H. (1961). *The Toadstool Millionaires: A Social History of Patent Medicines in America Before Federal Regulation*. Princeton University Press.

Zimmerman, D. L. (2006). The Story of Bleistein v. Donaldson Lithographing Company: Originality as a Vehicles for Copyright Inclusivity. In J. C. Ginsburg & R. C. Dreyfuss (Eds.), *Intellectual Property Stories* (pp. 77–106). Foundation Press.

CHAPTER 8

Early Twentieth-Century Trademarks and Brands

Abstract As trademark use expanded, a formal literature developed examining the concept then called trademark advertising. The idea of trademark advertising was that by advertising brand names to consumers, these consumers would then demand those brands from their retailers. This would reduce the power of retailers and wholesalers to select which products to stock. This also led to the development of the concept of a brand and consumer research examining brands.

Keywords Trademark advertising · Brand concept · Consumer research · Nabisco · Uneeda Biscuit · In-er-seal trademark · Shredded wheat

INTRODUCTION

If the later 1800s saw the popularization of brand marketing, the early 1900s saw its formalization (Petty, 2016, 105). Trademark law expanded to cover descriptive names that had acquired secondary meaning and trademark law shifted from unfair competition and passing off to the protection of property rights of brand owners (Petty, 2011). Because of their widespread use and growing trademark law enforcement, the period of 1915–1929 has been called the "Golden Age" of manufacturer brands

© The Author(s), under exclusive license to Springer Nature Switzerland AG 2024
R. D. Petty, *From Marking Products to Marketing Brands*, Palgrave Studies in Marketing, Organizations and Society,
https://doi.org/10.1007/978-3-031-76778-4_8

on consumer products. The total number of registered US trademarks grew from about 54,000 in 1906 to over 278,000 in 1930. The rate of annual trademark registrations increased eightfold from 1600 in 1900 to 13,000 in 1930.

As Petty (2011) notes, marketers and others recognized the additional value of technical trademarks over descriptive trade names during this period of trademark law and brand marketing development. Acheson (1917, 9) asserted "There is no more valuable and permanent property –if insured by continued publicity –than the trade mark of a staple commodity which has been well standardized by years of consistent advertising." Royal brand baking powder's goodwill in 1905 was valued at $5 million—a million dollars per letter (Pope, 1983, 69). In less than a decade Coca-Cola and Nabisco for its Uneeda brand were claiming similar valuations for their trademarks (Strasser, 1989, 47). Thus, the concept of what today would be called brand equity became recognized during this period.

THE CONCEPT OF TRADEMARK ADVERTISING

This excitement about technical trademarks led to the first known discussions of brand marketing using the term "trademark advertising." Perhaps the earliest discussion appears in a 1903 booklet entitled "The Value of Advertised Trademarks" by Ben B. Hampton Co., Advertising Agents that appears to be a reprint of material run in the trade journal, *Printers' Ink*. This work quotes from a graduation speech given by famous industrialist Andrew Carnegie: "If you can sell a hat for one dollar you can sell it for two dollars if you stamp it with your name and make the public feel that your name stands for something" (Hampton Co., 1903, 6). While Carnegie clearly understands the modern concept of brand marketing that a unique and protected name allows the marketer to promote what it "stands for," it is not clear whether he is thinking of "your name" as a personal name or a name you selected to brand your product.

Another candidate for the earliest discussion of "trademark advertising" is the J. Walter Thompson (JWT) advertisement published sometime in the mid-1900s. This advertisement explains the value of "trademark advertising"—if a firm advertises its technical trademark directly to consumers, they will request the brand by name from retailers. The advertiser will no longer be dependent on jobbers or retailers for brand promotion because the brand is now meaningful to consumers (Petty, 2011, 91; Schwarzkopf, 2010, 174). Direct-to-consumer advertising was not a new concept, but by tying advertising to the trademark, JWT was promoting brand marketing where the brand, rather than the marketer (in the past typically retailers), developed a direct relationship with its consumers (Fig. 8.1).

The English advertising agency of Spottiswoode, Dixon & Hunting, Ltd published a similar ad in the June 1907 issue of *The Strand Magazine* touting the antiquity of the trademark idea and its value in modern trade when it is advertised. In 1908, one advertising man estimated that "[a]t least fifty percent of advertising being done today is for the purpose of creating property in trademarks" (Pope, 1983, 69).

Petty (2011, 91–93) identifies several articles, pamphlets, and books that discuss the value of trademark advertising during the early 1900s. The books are listed by publication date and number of pages in Table 8.1.

The Development of the Brand Concept

Trademark advertising slowly evolved into brand marketing. Stern (2006, 217) claims "brand" entered the marketing lexicon in 1922 as part of the compound "brand name" but Bastos and Levy (2012, 353) suggest that the term brand was in common usage at least by 1920. They provide an example of a quote from P. T. Cherington (1920, 150): "the appeal to the buy... by brand has become so general as to be in many lines of merchandise the characteristic rather than the exception method of sale." Later in the same chapter entitled "Sales under Brand," Cherington (1920, 153) notes "The most common device for accomplishing this [appeal to the large mass of final consumers] is the use of a trade-mark or other means of identification."

Koehn (1999, 362) argues "brand" was a common term by turn-of-the-century. She notes that in 1890, the U.S. Supreme Court affirmed the dismissal of a trademark infringement dispute involving "Tycoon Tea" because these two words had been "in common use as a brand" for many years prior to the case. The Court held "Tycoon Tea" could not be appropriated as a trademark by a single firm (*Corbin v. Gould*, 1890, 313). She also presented two examples of economists' publications using "brand" in 1900–1901 (Beardsley, 1901, 85; Jenks, 1900, 29; Koehn, 1999, 362).

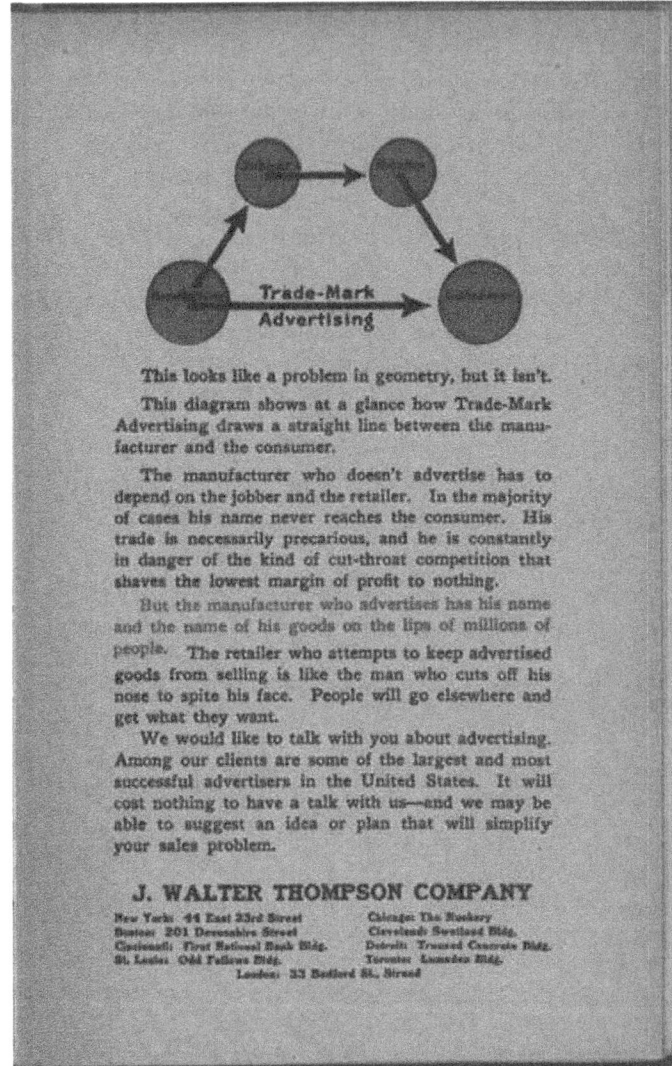

Fig. 8.1   J. Walter Thompson advertisement from Petty (2011, 91)

Table 8.1 Early Books about Trademark Advertising from Petty (2011, 92)

Year	Title	Author	Pages
1908	The Trademark: Its Value and How to Procure It	W. H. Black	24
1911	Things to Know About Trade-Marks	J. Walter Thompson	85
1912	Trade Marks, Trade Names for the Business Man	Munn & Co.	41
1915	Trade Marks, Trade Names and Unfair Competition in Trade	Orson D. Munn	76
1916	Trademark Power	Glen Buck	112
1917	Trade-Mark Advertising as an Investment	Arthur Acheson	46

The evolution from "trademark advertising" to "brand marketing" can be illustrated by looking at Cherington's earlier books. In *Advertising as a Business Force*, Cherington (1913, 331) does not yet offer a chapter on "Sales under Brand" but instead in a chapter entitled "Trade-Mark Problems" he notes: "The trade-mark has become one of the elements of almost every successful appeal to the consumer." He goes on to describe the trademark as a "commercial signature for its exploiter." In a nod to the notion of trademark advertising, he notes that the trademark has no intrinsic value but only produces business value if it is consistently advertised:

> The trade-mark, however, is only an emblem. It actually produces no business nor has it in itself any creative power. The value lies wholly in the action it inspires, its ability to suggest by continued appearance . . . Powerful, persistent publicity tends to invest an article with more value in the purchaser's mind who unconsciously associates it with merit and becomes predisposed in its favor. (Cherington, 1913, 332)

Thus, in this 1913 book, Cherington recognized the importance of the trademark advertising concept. In his second book, *The Advertising Book 1916*, he offers a chapter entitled "Trademarks and Brands" and presents numerous examples of the benefits of trademark advertising. He summarizes these arguments by quoting from a trade journal series of advertisements that concludes: "Trademarks and national advertising are the two greatest public servants in business to-day. Their whole tendency is to raise qualities and standardize them, while reducing prices and stabilizing them" (Cherington, 1916, 496). Thus, he still emphasizes trademark advertising but now ties it to brands and broadens the benefits from just sales to other consumer benefits. Four years later he announces the commonality of brand promotion enabled by protectable trademarks that is quoted at the beginning of this section.

Petty (2011, 92) notes that the literature continued during this period with general advertising books, including one published in the UK that may have been the first to use the word brand:

> The manufacturer advertises his brand direct to the public and thus liberates himself from entire dependence on the wholesaler's and retailer's goodwill ... [T]hese intermediaries can no longer afford not to stock what the ultimate consumer is asking by name as a consequence of the manufacture's advertising. Important features in the successful marketing of a proprietary article are a distinguishing name and mark, and, if practicable, a distinctive package or wrapping, so that substitution is difficult. (Goodall, 1914: 5, 48)

Three years later another US book, *Marketing Methods*, by Ralph Starr Butler (1917, 140–156) also used the term "brand" repeatedly in Chapter X "The Retailer and National Advertising." However, "brand' was not deemed sufficiently important to be included in the chapter title. Thus, by the mid-1910s, the concept of trademark advertising, itself only about ten years old, was being refined toward brand marketing. Inger Stole (2006, 20) notes: "By the 1920s, advertising had gone from being a peripheral business activity to a dominant force in U.S. life." As Cherington (1920) noted, advertising was predominantly brand-based at this time.

Consumer Research on Brands

Petty (2011, 93) notes that behavioral research conducted during this time also helped establish the intrinsic value of well-known brands. Advertising agencies like JWT were conducting research on why consumers bought particular brands and how they used them so that they could recommend both advertising copy and brand line extensions to reinforce and expand consumer behavior. Their advertising copy moved trademarks from decoration alone to brands with social meanings for consumers and personalities that lived in advertising and the minds of consumers. Thus, advertising agencies such as N. W. Ayer included registering new trademarks and promoting the brand identity as services offered during this time (Schwarzkopf, 2010, 170–176).

Not only was the concept of brand marketing developed by both marketing and legal experts, but its value was demonstrated by empirical studies of consumer beliefs. The very first volume of the *Journal of Applied Psychology* included an article on consumer brand associations with common products (Geissler, 1917). The article presented a study that developed data from 300 men from 8 different states where they were told a particular product category (that men were likely to buy themselves) and then asked to write down the first brand name that came to mind and the reason that brand came to mind. The most common reason for naming a particular brand was the consumer's personal evaluation of the brand. In nearly half the cases, this was based on use. The second most common reason was seeing that brand advertised.

The study concludes that brand advertising makes use more likely and of course use causes an even stronger bond between the consumer and brand making continued use even more likely. It empirically supports what the experts had been saying. Build a quality product, advertise it by brand name, and this will cause consumers to try the brand. Assuming good experience, they will become loyal to the brand.

This somewhat narrow study (twenty product categories) was further supported six years later by a book entitled *The Leadership of Advertised Brands* (Hotchkiss & Franken, 1923). This book examined 100 product categories and found that consumers on average could identify brands for about two-thirds of the product categories. Some brands were named by as many as 90% of all respondents. While recent research suggests this latter study overstates its conclusions, the critique also notes the results were widely reported and had a lasting impact on brand marketing literature (Golder, 2000). This suggests that the book and its results did indeed support the development of the brand marketing concept and showed that by this time, consumers were familiar with brands because brand marketing was commonplace.

Psychological studies of trademark infringement also were published in law reviews at this time (e.g., Burtt, 1925; Rogers, 1919). This work is built upon earlier studies of advertising effectiveness such as Gale (1900, 68). While his study did not include trademarks, he nonetheless concluded: "a plain statement in relevant words of the firm or name with the article, and in some permanent trademark form, is on the whole most effective for attention, combined with inducing real buying." Thus, brands through trademarks were recognized and proven to be effective as a tool to attract consumer interest as well as a property right of the owner—in essence, trademarks were valued because they communicated a brand identity rather than just the identity of the product source. Modern brand strategists recognize the importance of this distinction (Drescher, 1992).

During the 1930s, JWT continued using market research to develop branding strategies for Lever Brothers and Kraft (Mercer, 2010, 33). It went beyond brand identification and promotion to include research to understand a brand's existing "personality" and to use research to track attempts to change that personality. This focused development on emotional connections between consumers and brands enabled JWT to successfully rejuvenate the Lux brand during this time and would set the stage for much greater emphasis on brand personality in the 1950s (Schwarzkopf, 2010: 180–188). Similarly, the London firm of William Crawford was talking about "product personality" and the "advertising idea." The firm applied Dale Carnegies' concept of "winning friends and influencing people" to advertised brands (Schwarzkopf, 2009).

So brand marketers argued that the legal system needed to protect their efforts to invest in these trademarks through advertising expenditures that created brand meaning. Indeed advertisers at least in the US sought to have advertising expenditures treated as capital expenditures rather than short term business expenses for accounting and tax purposes. In addition, US courts looked beyond the amount of time a trademark had been in use to explicitly examine advertising expenditures to determine whether a descriptive mark had developed secondary meaning. (Bartholomew, 2008)

Trademark Evolution

As noted in previous chapters, the two major branches of law that protected brand identifiers from unauthorized imitation were trademark infringement and passing off as a form of unfair competition. Both of these approaches required proving that the unauthorized imitation occurred in the same or a closely related industry. Frank Schechter (1927), in a still famous *Harvard Law Review* article, argued that in cases of trademark use on non-competing products, while there is no trade diversion from the trademark owner, there would be "a gradual whittling away or dispersion of the identity and hold upon the public mind of the mark." He argued that protection against such trademark dilution should be provided for truly unique (arbitrary, coined, or fanciful) marks, but not for descriptive marks. He justified his proposal by arguing:

> ...today the trademark is not merely the symbol of good will but often the most effective agent for the creation of good will ... The mark actually *sells* the goods. And, self-evidently, the more distinctive the mark, the more effective is its selling power. (Schechter, 1927, 819) (emphasis in the original)

Despite this argument Schechter's proposal for a trademark dilution cause of action would not be accepted until the twenty-first century (Petty, 2011, 96).

Thus, it seems clear that the practice of modern brand marketing became popular in the latter 1800s, but the literature discussing the concept of brand marketing started in the early 1900s. This "Golden Age" also was the period where marketers began to develop the concept of brand managers that would be adopted by Proctor & Gamble in the early 1930s (Low & Fullerton, 1994, 177–180).

This shift to trademark advertising also led to a shift from factual to emotional advertising appeals. A recent study of print advertisements reported that advertisements based on logical appeals shrank from 62% in the1900s to 35% in the 1930s while emotionally appealing advertising increased from 27 to 42% of all product advertising during the same period (Pollay, 1986, 29). Even the U.S. Supreme Court noted that advertising created "commercial advertising" toward the brand (*Mishawaka Rubber & Woolen Mfg. Co. v. S.S. Kresge Co.*, 1942, 205).

Strasser (1989, 118) notes that character trademarks like the Campbell Kids (1906) experienced a "population explosion" in the U.S. beginning around 1900. Mendenhall (1990, 7) noted that "[a]round the turn of the century, companies started to recognize that personifying the products that they manufactured would be a valuable marketing tool." Richards (2022, 288, 289) lists eleven well-known characters that were used in the first decade of the twentieth century. Of course, as noted in the previous chapter, some character trademarks began their use in earlier times. For example, the Underwood Devil claimed first use in commerce in 1868 in its trademark registration filed in 1905.

Emotional propaganda campaigns also were used in World War I and considered successful leading to greater business interest in "scientific advertising" (Stole, 2006, 13–15). In response to this shift from rational to emotional appeals, courts started to adopt a less rational ordinary purchaser model of consumer behavior leading to trademark decisions seeking to protect "the ignorant, the unthinking and the credulous" from confusingly similar trademarks (*Florence Manufacturing Co. v. J.C. Dowd & Co.*, 1910, 75). However, as brand marketing and emotional or image advertising became well accepted, they also were criticized both by consumer groups and economists as discussed in the next chapter (Petty, 2011, 96).

Case Study: Nabisco

The National Biscuit Company was founded by attorney Adolpus W. Green in 1898, the product of a merger among the American Biscuit and Manufacturing Company, the New York Biscuit Company, and the United States Baking Company. The new cracker trust was headquartered in New York City and controlled over half of the cracker and cookie business in America, with 114 bakeries and over 400 ovens, producing 360 million pounds of crackers a year (Hoover, 2021). Over the next several decades the company grew by acquiring companies such as the Shredded Wheat Company, maker of Triscuit Wafers, and Shredded Wheat Cereal.

It also grew by selling snacks packaged and branded for consumer purchase to diversify from just selling crackers in bulk. The Uneeda Biscuit (U.S. Trademark Reg. No. 32301, registered in 1898), National Biscuit Company's first packaged cracker, was the subject of the company's first million-dollar advertising campaign (totaling $7 million in the first decade). This campaign sold 100 million boxes by 1900 when consumers bought 10 million packages monthly (5 cents each). It was called a biscuit—the British term for cracker to denote a more upscale product than a cracker sold in a large barrel (and sometimes stale or soggy at "the bottom of the barrel") (Cross, 2002, 20–22; Kahn, 1969, 70).

In addition to the catchy name, Uneeda became well known for its In-er-Seal packaging and its In-er-Seal trademark symbol (Reg. No. 35108, registered in 1900). In 1899, Frank Peters invented a box made with cardboard lined with wax paper as well as a method to produce the box (Reg. No. 621974). He sought a patent to cover both and was surprised when one was issued. He licensed the entire patent to National Biscuit. The In-er-Seal packaging enabled the biscuits to stay crispy longer than the traditional crackers sold in a cracker barrel so could be shipped and consumers trusted its fresh crispiness. Unfortunately for Peters and National Biscuit, the patent was declared invalid and unenforceable in November 1903 for lacking "patentable novelty." Many were already using cardboard containers with wax paper linings (Kahn, 1969, 116–117; *Union Biscuit Co. v. Peters*, 1903, 607). However, National Biscuit continued to use and enforce its In-er-Seal trademark symbol.

A third prong was added to National Biscuit's campaign to sell Uneeda Biscuits after February 1901, when National Biscuit took the first picture of five-year-old Gordon Stille as the National Biscuit "slicker boy." This series of ads, where the boy carefully displays the product name on the top of the box and the In-er-Seal symbol on the end of the box, both promoted product performance that the In-er-Seal system would keep Uneeda biscuits crisp and promoted brand image. The innocent boy as a character trademark offered a view of warm Americana so customers would feel good about the brand. His image was used in a $7 million advertising campaign to sell more than 10 million packages per month in 1900. Other packaged crackers sold about half a million packages per year (Kahn, 1969, 92). In the early twentieth century, his image was the second most recognized in the country after the U.S. President (Inner Seal Collectors Club, n.d.) (Fig. 8.2).

Success brought imitation and A. W. Green, the attorney running the company, was not about to let imitations go unchallenged. For example, in two well-publicized court decisions in 1899, Nabisco was recognized

I will call
prepared to
take orders
for

**Uneeda
Biscuit**

and other

Crackers
on or about

Resp'fully
yours

Copyright 1902, NATIONAL BISCUIT COMPANY

NATIONAL BISCUIT COMPANY

Fig. 8.2 The "Slicker Boy." From: https://americanbusinesshistory.org/une eda-business-history-the-nabisco-story/

as having a valid trademark, Uneeda Biscuit, and received an injunction against use of the trademark and similar packaging graphics by two competitors selling Uwanta and Iwanta Biscuit (Kahn, 1969, 114–115; National Biscuit Company, 1915, 5–18). Eleven similar cases were litigated through 1915 (Fig. 8.3).

Fig. 8.3 Legal challenges from Nabisco by Year (National Biscuit Company, 1915)

The total 13 litigated successes against imitators allowed National Biscuit to credibly threaten other imitators (as many as 200 in 1908) so they would stop without litigation. Some of these cases involved formal injunctions or the payment of damages. There were consistently more challenges to imitators of the In-er-Seal trademark than the Uneeda trademark because the former was used on other products (National Biscuit Company, 1915).

Table 8.1 Trademark disputes in which National Biscuit obtained abandonment of imitation In-er-Seal and Uneeda trademarks by year. Derived from National Biscuit Company (1915, 233).

Of course, National Biscuit was not always successful with litigation. In the early 1920s, it challenged three different bakeries attempting to register "Hava," "O-Such-A," and "Eta" as applied to biscuits. The Trademark Office allowed registration in all three examples but was reversed on appeal resulting in the denial of trademark registration of "Eta." The other two registrations were affirmed (*National Biscuit Co. v. Bishop & Co.*, 1923; *National Biscuit Co. v. Pennsylvania Baking Co.*, 1923; *National Biscuit Co. v. J. B. Carr Biscuit Co.*, 1924).

National Biscuit faced one additional and important battle involving alleged unfair competition. In December 1928, it acquired the Shredded Wheat Company, the original producer of shredded wheat whose patent expired in 1912. The Company had been struggling with various attempts by Kellogg to produce its own shredded wheat product. Two years after acquiring Shredded Wheat, National Biscuit brought its lawsuit for unfair competition (Dinwoodie, 2005; Kahn, 1969, 218–220).

After proceedings in about a dozen different tribunals in the U.S. and England, the U.S. Supreme Court would decide this case in 1938 (Kahn, 1969, 220; *Kellogg Co. v. National Biscuit Co.*, 1938). The court of appeals found in favor of the Shredded Wheat Company, but the Supreme Court overturned that decision. The Court held that the pillow shape of the biscuits was functional and non-distinctive (without mentioning

Fig. 8.4 From https://beachpackagingdesign.com/boxvox/shredded-wheat-documents-cereal-as-intellectual-property

expired design patents each party had been issued that suggests the shape was primarily ornamental not functional). Furthermore, since the utility and design patents had expired, there was a right for anyone to copy the invention. Lastly, the Court held that the term "shredded wheat" had become generic with the patent expirations so any imitator like Kellogg could use "shredded wheat" so long as the source of the imitation product was clearly identified (Fig. 8.4).

National Biscuit officially became the Nabisco Company in 1971. In addition to Uneeda Biscuit, discontinued in 2009, the company developed and still sells Ritz Crackers, Oreos, Sugar Wafers, and Animal Crackers among other products. In 1993, the Shredded Wheat Company was sold to Kraft that discontinued the Nabisco name on that product in 1999. It is now sold under the Post brand in the U.S.

REFERENCES

Acheson, A. (1917). *Trade-Mark Advertising as an Investment*. Evening Post.

Bartholomew, M. (2008). Advertising and the Transformation of Trademark Law. *New Mexico Law Review, 38*(1), 1–48.

Bastos, W., & Levy, S. J. (2012). A History of the Concept of Branding: Practice and Theory. *Journal of Historical Research in Marketing, 14*(3), 347–368.

Beardsley, C. (1901). The Tariff and the Trusts. *Quarterly Journal of Economics, 15*(3), 371–389.

Burtt, H. E. (1925). Measurement of Confusion Between Similar Trade Names. *Illinois Law Review, 19*, 320–342.

Butler, R. S. (1917). *Marketing Methods.* Alexander Hamilton Institute.

Cherington, P. T. (1913). *Advertising as a Business Force.* Doubleday, Page & Co.

Cherington, P. T. (1916). *The Advertising Book 1916.* Doubleday, Page & Co.

Cherington, P. T. (1920). *The Elements of Marketing.* The Macmillan Co.

Corbin v. Gould (1890). 133 U.S. 308.

Cross, M. (2002). *A Century of American Icons.* Greenwood Press.

Dinwoodie, G. B. (2005). The Story of Kellogg v. National Biscuit Company: Breakfast with Brandeis. In R. Dreyfuss & J. Ginsburg (Eds), *Intellectual Property Stories* (pp. 220–257). Foundation Press.

Drescher, T. D. (1992). The Transformation and Evolution of Trademarks: From Signals to Symbols to Myth. *Trademark Reporter, 82*(3), 301–340.

Florence Manufacturing Co. v. J.C. Dowd & Co., (1910) 178 Fed. 73 (C.C.A).

Gale, H. (1900). On the Psychology of Advertising. In H. Gale (Ed.), *Psychological Studies* (pp. 36–69). University Press.

Geissler, L. R. (1917). Association—Reactions Applied to Ideas of Commercial Brands of Familiar Articles. *Journal of Applied Psychology, 1*(3), 275–290. https://doi.org/10.1037/h0074861

Golder, P. N. (2000). Historical Method in Marketing Research with New Evidence on Long-Term Market Share Stability. *Journal of Market Research, 37*(2), 156–172. https://doi.org/10.1509/jmkr.37.2.156.18732

Goodall, G. W. (1914). *Advertising: A Study of a Modern Business Power.* Constable & Co.

Hampton Co. B. B. (1903). *The Value of Advertised Trademarks.* Ben B. Hampton Co.

Hoover, G. (2021). *Uneeda Business History: the Nabisco Story.* American Business History Center. Retrieved July 25, 2024 from https://americanbusines shistory.org/uneeda-business-history-the-nabisco-story/

Hotchkiss, G. B., & Franken, R. B. (1923). *The Leadership of Advertised Brands; A Study of 100 Representative Commodities Showing the Names and Brands That Are Most Familiar to the Public.* Doubleday, Page & Company.

Inner Seal Collectors Club. (n.d.). *About.* https://nationalbiscuitcollectors.wor dpress.com/about/

Jenks, J. W. (1900). *The Trust Problem.* Doubleday, Page & Company.

Kahn, W. (1969). *Out of the Cracker Barrel: The Nabisco Story from Animal Crackers to Zuzus.* Simon & Schuster.

Kellogg Co. v. National Biscuit Co. (1938). 305 U.S. 111.

Koehn, N. F. (1999). Henry Heinz and Brand Creation in the Late Nineteenth Century: Making Markets for Processed Food. *Business History Review, 73*(Autumn), 349–393.

Low, G. S., & Fullerton, R. A. (1994). Brands, Brand Management, and the Brand Manager System: A Critical-Historical Evaluation. *Journal of Marketing Research, 31*(2), 173–190.

Mendenhall, J. (1990). *Character Trademarks*. Chronicle Books.

Mercer, J. (2010). A Mark of Distinction: Branding and Trade Mark Law in the UK from the 1860s. *Business History, 52*(1), 17–42.

Mishawaka Rubber & Woolen Mfg. Co. v. S.S. Kresge Co. (1942)., 316 U.S. 203 (U.S. Supreme Court).

National Biscuit Company. (1915). *Trademark Litigation*. National Biscuit Company.

National Biscuit Co. v. Bishop & Co. (1923). 286 F. 464 (C.A.D.C.).

National Biscuit Co. v. J. B. Carr Biscuit Co. (1924). 3 F.2d 87 (C.A.D.C.)

National Biscuit Co. v. Pennsylvania Baking Co. (1923). 285 F, 1018 (C.A.D.C.).

Petty, R. D. (2011). The Co-development of Trademark Law and the Concept of Brand Marketing in the U.S. Before 1946. *Journal of Macromarketing, 31*(1), 85–99.

Petty, R. D. (2016). A History of Brand Identity Protection and Brand Marketing. In B. D. G. Jones & M. Tadajewski (Eds.), *The Routledge Companion to Marketing History* (pp. 76–114). Routledge.

Pollay, R. W. (1986). The Distorted Mirror: Reflections on the Unintended Consequences of Advertising. *Journal of Marketing, 50*(2), 18–36. https://doi.org/10.1177/002224298605000202

Pope, D. (1983). *The Making of Modern Advertising*. Basic Books.

Richards, J. I. (2022). *A History of Advertising: The First 300,000 Years*. Bowman & Littlefield.

Rogers, E. S. (1919). An Account of Some Psychological Experiments on the Subject of Trade-Mark Infringement. *Michigan Law Review, 18*(2), 75–103.

Schechter, F. I. (1927). The Rational Basis of Trademark Protection. *Harvard Law Review, 40*(6), 813–833.

Schwarzkopf, S. (2009). What Was Advertising? The Invention, Rise, Demise, and Disappearance of Advertising Concepts in Nineteenth- and Twentieth-Century Europe and America. *Business and Economic History Online, 7,* 1–27. https://thebhc.org/sites/default/files/schwarzkopf.pdf

Schwarzkopf, S. (2010). Turning Trademarks into Brands: How Advertising Agencies Practiced and Conceptualized Branding, 1890–1930. In T. da Silva Lopes & P. Duguid (Eds.), *Trademarks, Brands, and Competitiveness* (pp. 165–193). Routledge.

Stern, B. B. (2006). What Does Brand Mean? Historical-Analysis Method and Construct Definition. *Journal of the Academy of Marketing Science, 23*(2), 216–223.

Stole, I. L. (2006). *Advertising on Trial: Consumer Activism and Corporate Public Relations in the 1930s.* University of Illinois Press.

Strasser, S. (1989). *Satisfaction Guaranteed: The Making of the American Mass Market.* Pantheon Books.

Union Biscuit Co. v. Peters (1903). 125 F. 601 (8th Cir.).

Wilcox, C. (1934). Brand Names, Quality, and Price. *The Annals of the American Academy of Political and Social Science, 173*(1), 80–85.

CHAPTER 9

Criticism of Brand Marketing (1920–1946)

Abstract The early 1900s advocates in the consumer movement criticized brand marketing for its large amount of advertising leading to higher prices and its lack of transparency concerning product information regarding attributes and performance. This led economists to study both the imperfect competition caused by brand marketing and the economic effects of advertising. The Federal Trade Commission was established in 1914. While it did not attack brand marketing directly at this time, it, as well as the Food & Drug Administration, did pursue companies that used misleading brand names and occasionally required information that was needed by consumers to make informed product choices.

Keywords "Victory" brand bicycles · Consumer movement · Federal Trade Commission · Food & Drug Administration

The total number of registered US trademarks grew from about 54,000 in 1906 to over 278,000 in 1930. Annual trademark registrations increased eightfold from 1600 in 1900 to 13,000 in 1930. This growth in registered brand identifiers fueled growth in advertising that featured trademarks. "By the 1920s, advertising had gone from being a peripheral business activity to a dominant force in U.S. life" (Stole, 2006, 20).

© The Author(s), under exclusive license to Springer Nature Switzerland AG 2024
R. D. Petty, *From Marking Products to Marketing Brands*, Palgrave Studies in Marketing, Organizations and Society,
https://doi.org/10.1007/978-3-031-76778-4_9

Annual advertising expenditures increased fivefold from $542 million in 1900 to $3.4 billion in 1929 (Fox, 1997, 118; Stole, 2006, 20–22). As advertising exposure increased, it also shifted to a decrease of informational content to an increase of emotional appeals and imagery for brands protected by trademarks (Mayer, 1989, 20).

Yet despite brand marketing's popularity, there were still those who opposed it. It was well recognized that brand marketing involved expensive advertising and promotion and the prices of branded products were higher than comparable unbranded products. For example, studies showed that branded foods sold for 50–60% more than foods bought in bulk during this time (Wilcox, 1934, 84). As products became more standardized, critics questioned whether brand marketing was worth the higher prices for essentially the same products. Not surprisingly, this concern increased during the Great Depression of the 1930s (Petty, 2018).

Background: The Early Consumer Movement

In the early1900s, a consumer movement (Mayer, 1989; Petty, 2015, 530–531; Stole, 2006, 58–62) developed that would later lead to brand marketing criticism. The movement's initial concerns were food and drug safety and misleading claims about safety or performance. After years of debate, Congress finally passed the 1906 Pure Food and Drugs Act that created the modern Food and Drug Administration out of the Bureau of Chemistry of the Department of Agriculture. Although primarily focused on food and drug safety and product standards, this law outlawed any food that was "an imitation of or offered for sale under the distinctive name of another article." While this provision was intended to apply to standard food names such as jelly which was commonly half fruit and half sugar, it might also be applied to distinctive brand names.

For example, a product called Bred-Spred would have been considered adulterated or misbranded jelly under the FDA's standards because it had no fruit. "But because the name was distinctive name–it didn't call itself jam or jelly–manufacturers had legal protection from misbranding charges." This defense encouraged the development of distinctive food brand names that might mislead consumers about the contents of the branded product. The defense would be repealed in 1938.

Hess (1922) suggests that interest in truth-in-advertising started around 1893 but solidified in 1911 when legal expert H.D. Nims explained why proving damages under existing laws made it difficult to control false advertising through either the civil common law or existing criminal law of false pretenses. Nims proposed a model statute (commonly known as the Printers' Ink Model Statute) that was adopted in 37 states (Cole, 1921, 20; Wood, 1958, 336). These laws would be primarily enforced voluntarily by local advertising clubs and Better Business Bureaus under the threat of possible prosecution (Petty, 2015, 530–531).

In 1914 when US advertising expenditures are estimated to be around $1.1 billion (Richards, 2022, 232), the Federal Trade Commission (FTC) was formed as an independent regulatory agency empowered to define and prohibit unfair methods of competition that would include false advertising for nearly all products. Brown (1947, 194–199) suggests that between 1920 and 1934, courts were not receptive to FTC condemnations of advertising exaggeration but were supportive of cases (similar to trademark infringement cases) where one type of goods was being "passed off" as another type such as non-wool garments advertised as though they were wool or contained wool. Brown's (1947) analysis of decisions also indicated that the courts became more supportive of the FTC over time.

In addition to pursuing misleading advertising generally, the FTC also began to address the criticism that brand marketing emphasized brand or misdescriptive trade names over factual information so that consumers struggled to obtain accurate factual information about product attributes, grades, or performance. In 1918, the FTC met with marketers of gold-plated finger rings in order to create a standard for describing gold content that would allow consumers to compare the gold value of rings. The Commission could then pursue jewelers who did not follow these standards (Chase & Schlink, 1927, 103–105). This appears to be the first Commission effort to provide a standardized information disclosure that would allow consumers to compare the quality of competing products.

From this industry meeting evolved what soon would be known as the Trade Practice Conference. Between 1919 and 1934, the Commission held 164 Conferences and approved rules regarding fair and unfair competition for 150 of them which sometimes called for the provision of product information (Gaskill, 1936, 106–112; Kittelle & Mastow, 1940, 428–435). However, this program stopped when the development of codes was criticized in the mid-1930s for contributing to price rigidity and high prices (Jacobs, 2005, 130).

CRITICISM OF BRAND MARKETING

As the consumer movement evolved, it went beyond criticizing misleading advertising to develop a critique of brand marketing itself. Stuart Chase and Frederick J. Schlink wrote *Your Money's Worth: A Study in the Waste of Consumer's Dollars* in 1927. *Your Money's Worth* has been called the *Uncle Tom's Cabin* of the consumer movement. Within ten years, it had sold an estimated 100,000 copies (Stole, 2006, 23, 174).

Your Money's Worth criticized many advertising practices for being misleading or uninformative. Specifically, the book argued that most brand advertising failed to give consumers sufficient product information leading consumers to buy goods they otherwise would not have purchased. Attractive packaging and "shining up the article" also can be used to enhance an offering's purchase appeal by distracting focus from the attributes of the actual product itself. Chase and Schlink argued that brand marketing limited competition" (1927, 166). They quoted an advertisement by a famous advertising agency:

> The final purpose of advertising is not to prove the comparative superiority of the article in competition. The object of advertising is to TAKE IT OUT OF COMPETITION, that it will no longer be compared but will be accepted by the buyer'. (Emphasis in the original)

Chase and Schlink (1927, 164–166) offer five specific critiques of the "brand system." First, they denounce the growth of substantially identical brands "without limit so long as advertising pressure is capable of creating demand" in part to satisfy the desire of each marketing agent to have its own exclusive brand. Second, they bemoan the technical complexity of many modern products and note that brand advertising tends to make even simple products appear too complex for the ordinary consumer to understand. Third, brand advertising surrounds simple products with a "halo of characteristics" that don't exist or don't contribute to product performance but nevertheless sound important.

Fourth, they argue brands are no guarantee of consistent quality because brand marketers are free to change and often do change their formulae and product characteristics. They specifically note that new brands of cigarettes decrease their quality after becoming well accepted by consumers. Fifth and finally, brand packaging thwarts consumer analysis by weights and measures so that some branded products are priced dramatically higher for any given quantity than their unbranded alternatives. Brands were not priced to the cost of production but rather were priced at whatever level "the traffic will bear" (Chase & Schlink, 1927, 17, 164).

This condemnation of the "brand system" appears to accept the practice of brand identification instead challenging brand promotion to the exclusion of providing functional information about product performance. Chase and Schlink (1927) proposed regulation to standardize products with certified levels of quality so that standardized language would be used to discuss product attributes and performance as well as the quantity provided. This additional information would allow consumers to make well-reasoned and informed choices about the brands they buy (Petty, 2011, 95). This book and others became part of a consumer movement that led to private product testing by consumers groups and truth-in-advertising reform rather than any changes in the scope of trademark law (Stole, 2006).

Chase and Schlink's (1927) popular critique of brand marketing was followed by similar academic economic analysis. Braithwaite (1928) considered brand advertising to be a selling cost that was used to persuade consumers to more highly value the advertised brand. This created a reputation for the brand that could force rivals to spend even more money on advertising in order to overcome the reputation of the established brand and create a reputation for the new brand. Advertising brands allowed firms to create "reputational monopolies." While such reputations can act as a guarantee of quality for consumers there also is a risk of reputations being created for inferior goods if consumers can't readily evaluate the product quality for themselves. Sadly, this early analysis and critique of brand marketing has been largely forgotten today (Bagwell, 2005, 10).

From a consumer interest perspective, the timing of *Your Money's Worth* could not have been better. Within two years of its publication, the October 1929 stock market crash led to the Great Depression, causing unemployment approaching 30% and enhanced consumer price sensitivity and reticence to purchase higher priced branded products. By 1933, advertising expenditures were less than half of the $2 billion they reached in 1929 (Stole, 2006, 32). Trademark registrations also slowed from 13,000 in 1930 to about 10,000 per year in the decade of the 1930s. To stem these declines, the trade journal *Advertising Age* advocated that brand advertising acted as an assurance of quality for consumers and they should continue to buy branded products (*Advertising Age*, 1932, 1934).

Despite these industry-re-assurances, brand marketing continued to be criticized.

BRAND MARKETING AND PRICE COMPETITION

In the middle of the Great Depression, two economists published books in 1933 proposing economic models that explained why branded products were shielded to some degree from price competition. The first book was published by Edward Chamberlin (1933) and based on his PhD thesis on monopolistic competition that was completed in 1927 when Schechter (1927) was advocating for greater trademark protection in the *Harvard Law Review* and Chase and Schlink (1927) published *Your Money's Worth.* Joan Robinson (1933) published the second book soon thereafter. These books would begin an extensive scholarly discussion of the economics of advertising (Bagwell, 2005).

Both Chamberlin (1933) and Robinson (1933) argued that competition among differentiated products was imperfect (i.e., monopolistic) because such products enjoyed some level of monopoly power over their specific brand. They could charge prices higher than the competitive level. However, this brand monopoly power was limited to some degree by competition from other brands so the system was not as harmful as a complete monopoly with no competition at all.

Chamberlin (1933) specifically discussed trademarks (often comparing them to patents) as the enabler of product differentiation that allowed for monopolistic competition. He recognized that brand advertising could allow a brand to take advantage of economies of scale and reduce prices or it could raise costs and make the brand demand curve less elastic to increase prices (Chamberlin, 1933, 165–167). Similarly, Robinson (1933, 101) argued that if a market becomes uncomfortably competitive, a firm "can resort to advertisement and other devices which attach customers more firmly to itself."

The following year, Consumer Research advisor and economics professor Colston E. Warne (1934) synthesized critiques of brand marketing down to two fundamental criticisms that would drive the battle against brand marketing for the next fifty years. First, brand advertising had to promote the appeal of the brand itself in order to differentiate brands of similar products from each other and persuade consumers to pay a price premium for branded goods. The higher prices enabled marketers to afford more brand-differentiating advertising.

Second, because of its focus on the brand instead of the product, brand advertising contains too little product information for consumers to make an informed product selection (Warne, 1934, 71). This emphasis of brand over product quality and performance also was noted by Swarthmore College economist Clair Wilcox (1934) who disagreed with *Advertising Age* that consumers could rely on advertised brands as an assurance of quality:

> Brands are convenient.... Buying by brand is no substitute for buying on the basis of comparative prices and standard specifications. Its [brand marketing's] costs, in general, are far in excess of its worth. (Wilcox, 1934, 85)

He also argued brand pricing was more rigid than commodity pricing and therefore would prolong economic recovery.

THE CONSUMER MOVEMENT CONTINUES

During his 1932 presidential campaign, President Roosevelt predicted that the consumer would gain importance in the future (Cohen, 2003). The very next year, consumer advocates and others began work on new statutes to address perceived loopholes in the 1906 Federal Food and Drug Act. The original Copeland bill would have authorized grades and standards for all food and condemned ads that were misleading because of implication or ambiguity (Fox, 1997, 125). However, the 1938 Food, Drug, and Cosmetic Act was less sweeping. It eliminated the 1906 provision protecting the use of "distinctive names" and replaced it with authorization for the FDA to establish three types of food standards: identity, quality, and package fill (Chen, 1992). Food marketers must label their product with its standard name and conform to FDA standards (Mayer, 1989, 24). Of course, they still could also use a non-misleading brand name.

1938 also saw amendments to the FTC Act to address misleading advertising by authorizing it to pursue "unfair or deceptive acts or practices" (Mayer, 1989, 25; Stole, 2006, 138–158). One early proposal on misleading advertising would condemn "all representations of fact or opinion" that by "ambiguity or inference created a false or misleading impression" about foods or drugs (Stole, 2006, 54). However, the advertising community opposed such regulations directed at the alleged emotional and non-informational advertising of brands. They substituted their own proposals that would only condemn misstatements of facts and presumably allow puffery, omission of important facts, and emotional appeals to continue unregulated (Stole, 2006, 55–56).

As the FDA's pursued mislabeled food, the FTC challenged misleading brand names. In 1929, the Third Circuit Federal Court of Appeals affirmed an FTC ruling prohibiting the use of the trade name Duraleather to sell artificial leather products, even when accompanied by the phrase "durable leather substitute" (*Masland Duraleather Co. v. FTC*, 1929). However, four years later, the Supreme Court held that before excising valuable trade names, the FTC had to consider whether a disclosure remedy would cure the deceptiveness of the trade name without completely prohibiting its use (*FTC v. Royal Milling Co.*, 1933; *Jacob Siegel Co. v. FTC*, 1946). Despite this limitation, the FTC continued to pursue misleading brand names through World War II (*Ritz Distributors Corp. v. FTC*, 1944) and beyond (*Arrow Metal Products Corp. v. FTC*, 1957).

ECONOMIC STUDIES OF BRAND ADVERTISING

Debates about the 1938 consumer protection statutes caused the Advertising Research Foundation to propose in 1937 that the Harvard Business School undertake a comprehensive impartial study of the economic effects of advertising. The result was the 1942 book of the same name as this subject by Neil H. Borden (1942, p. vii). This study concluded that advertising tends to improve the quality and range of merchandise available to consumers by encouraging the adoption of major inventions and stimulating minor product improvements in pursuit of brand differentiation and the better satisfaction of consumer desires. The study also found that consumers benefit from the brand marketer's desire to maintain high product quality to maintain the brand's reputation and goodwill.

Borden conceded that product differentiation was a series of experiments by marketers to see what most appeals to consumers. Even modest distinctions between branded products can be important to some consumers (Borden, 1942, 866–868). He further noted that while brand advertising was an expense that is difficult for new entrants to match, some enter with a low-price strategy, e.g., retail private label or unbranded products. In the case of a new product, advertising is necessary to explain the benefits to consumers to induce purchase (Borden, 1942, 871–874).

This same year, Helen Canoyer (1942) also published a study of national brand advertising in the *Journal of Marketing*. She concluded that heavy advertising did not necessarily lead to concentration of production into a few firms. In addition, brand use and recall, occurring after advertising, may allow producers to sell products at a high price but did not lead to any single firm controlling all or even most of the supply of goods.

At the same time as Borden's (1942) private study, Congress created the Temporary National Economic Committee (TNEC) to study whether economic concentration was causing a decline in competition by either enabling price control or by the use of marketing practices such as a high level of advertising to stabilize the market and prices. Between 1939 and 1941, TNEC engaged over 180 experts and spent more than one million dollars to examine 95 different industries, hear from 552 witnesses to produce 43 monographs and 37 volumes of testimony (Stole, 2012, 20–22).

The Committee found that the degree to which brand advertising insulated products from price competition varied depending on the product and how readily buyers could compare the various qualities of the brand offerings. Thus, in some markets, a small price difference would cause consumers to switch brands, but in other markets, consumers could not evaluate product attributes so they relied upon brands and were less sensitive to price changes (Temporary National Economic Committee, 1941, 76–77).

The TNEC heard testimony on how advertising could prevent new products from entering a market or at least force a new marketer to match advertising budgets of existing firms. The Committee also heard testimony that advertising was not providing sufficient information to enable consumers to buy intelligently and therefore standardized product grading was needed. The consumer movement was now resigned to the continuation of brand marketing but argued that the provision of quality information from grading standards could help consumers get the most value for their money and stimulate price competition (Stole, 2012, 81–83). Occasionally, business executives such as Arthur Price of Sears Roebuck supported quality grading because that was what many consumers were requesting (Newman, 2004, 157).

CASE STUDY: VICTORY "BRAND" BICYCLES

When the US entered World War II, TNEC dissolved and the Office of Price Administration and Civilian Supply began rationing supplies and controlling prices (Stole, 2012, 32, 73). While comparing prices with authorized ceilings was relatively straightforward, the government struggled to check the large variety of products to make sure they were in appropriate price categories. To address the issue of product variety and matching quality levels with appropriate price ceilings, a standards division was created within OPA in the early fall of 1942. By January 1943, the division had reduced sizes and styles of certain consumer and industrial goods from 12,000 to 3,400 (Mezerik, 1943, 65; Stole, 2012, 83–85). Reducing variety would lower costs of production and allow more resources to be directed toward the war effort.

Brand marketers were concerned not only about product standardization and grading but also with the government's plan to prohibit the production of some branded consumer products during the war. These branded products would be replaced by a limited production and sales of standardized unbranded "Victory" products. The goal of this program was to allocate scarce materials primarily to the war effort, but not provide an unfair advantage to the few firms (and their brands) selected to produce civilian products. The classic example of this program was the Victory bicycle. Just ten days after Japan attacked Pearl Harbor in December 1941, the U.S. government announced that it would control bicycle production during the war (Longhurst, 2015, 131).

In March 1942, the government began its bicycle program by banning further production of children's bicycles but allowing an increase in production of adult bicycles over past levels. However, the next month, the War Production Board froze all bicycle production and sales for civilian use. By July, the WPB had determined that only 750,000 new bikes for both civilian and military use would be built annually by two (Huffman and Westfield) of the twelve companies that previously produced bicycles. Other bike companies, such as Schwinn, would produce munitions instead of bicycles. The new bikes would be standardized adult bicycles lighter in weight and with narrower tires than the balloon-tired models that were popular before the war and with limited use of chrome and no accessories such as baskets or bells. This model would sell for $32.50 on the east coast and would not be branded but only labeled as a Victory bicycle.

In August 1942, the WPB stopped all bicycle production but continued to ration existing inventory until September 1944. In May 1945, the WPB lifted all restrictions on the manufacture of bicycles. By that time about 96,000 Victory bicycles had been produced for civilian use (Fitzpatrick, 2011, 171–174; Longhurst, 2015, 120–124, 130–151).

In 1942, the *Wall Street Journal* described this program as a "tip-off of how trademarks and trade names will be handled as the manufacture of civilian goods is concentrated in fewer factories." However, the article further noted that there was no prohibition on wartime advertising of the unavailable pre-war bicycle brands "to keep their trade names alive" (*Wall Street Journal*, 1942). The article further noted that the program could spread to other consumer durable products but only a few industries were currently being considered for the program. The Mattress industry also sold "Victory" brand mattresses as several industry members were converted to produce munitions (Duncan 1944). Brand marketers and the advertising industry were afraid that this Victory label substituting for trademarked brand names would become the wartime norm in multiple industries.

It did not. While the bicycle industry complied with the Victory program, the canned food industry led the battle against grading and obtained legislative relief in 1943 that made it illegal for OPA to require grade labeling on any commodity. Products could be standardized only if OPA determined that no other method of price control was practicable. This led to the repeal of some grade labeling requirements for about twenty products. This 1943 statutory amendment also prohibited OPA from eliminating or restricting the use of trade or brand names because of some concerns that grade labeling was an attack on brand marketing which some perceived as essential to the economic well-being of the nation (Stole, 2012, 90–91). Thus, as Mezerik (1943) noted, consumers often preferred known brands. For example, they continued to pay a few cents more for the Squibb brand U.S.P. standard Epsom salts even though lower priced salts that met the same U.S.P. standard were available.

In 1944, a new "educational organization"—the Brand Names Research Foundation joined other marketing organizations opposed to OPA's renewal and grade labeling proposals. Many consumers, such as African Americans, were strongly in favor of both because they felt exploited with low-quality products during the war (Cohen, 2003, 86–87). Consumer groups failed to get either initiative enacted and with the demise of OPA in 1946, the Foundation continued advocating trade-marks and brand names as the core of the American economic system in opposition to consumer and labor groups that sought regulation of brand marketing (McGovern 2006). In 1947, it held two important events—the Brand Names Day conference and a 15 day festival called the Brand Names Celebration in Greenfield Massachusetts both extolling the importance of mass-produced brand-name products. These events would be repeated in future years as part of the Foundation's efforts to educate Americans about the benefits of brand marketing (Spring, 2011, 47–67).

References

Advertising Age. (1932). Advertised Brands as a Protection to the Consumer. *Advertising Age, 3*(31), 4.

Advertising Age. (1934). Consumers Have Faith in Advertising. *Advertising Age, 5*(3), 4.

Arrow Metal Products Corp. v. FTC (1957), 249 F.2d 83 (3rd Cir.).

Bagwell, K. (2005). *The Economic Analysis of Advertising* (Columbia University Department of Economics Discussion Paper No.: 0506-01). https://academ iccommons.columbia.edu/catalog/ac:115358. Accessed 12 July 2017.

Borden, N. H. (1942). *The Economic Effects of Advertising*. Irwin.

Braithwaite, D. (1928). The Economic Effects of Advertisement. *Economic Journal, 38*(149), 16–37.

Brown, W. F. (1947). The Federal Trade Commission and False Advertising II. *Journal of Marketing, 12*(2), 193–201.

Canoyer, H. G. (1942). National Brand Advertising and Monopolistic Competi-tion. *Journal of Marketing, 7*(2), 152–157.

Chamberlin, E. H. (1933). *The Theory of Monopolistic Competition*. Harvard University Press.

Chase, S., & Schlink, F. J. (1927). *Your Money's Worth: A Study in the Waste of the Consumer's Dollar*. The Macmillan Co.

Chen, C. (1992). Food and Drug Administration Food Standards of Identity: Consumer Protection Through the Regulation of Product Information. *Food and Drug Law Journal, 47*(2), 185–206.

Cohen, L. (2003). *A Consumers' Republic: The Politics of Mass Consumption in Postwar America*. Knopf.

Cole, R. (1921). Review of the Ten-Year Fight Against Fraudulent Advertising-II. *Printers' Ink, 114*(9), 121–130.

Duncan, G. B. (1944, July 22). Bedding Business. *Wall Street Journal*, 1, 2.

Fitzpatrick, J. (2011). *The Bicycle in Wartime: An Illustrated History* (Rev. Ed.). Star Hill Studio PTY, Ltd.

Fox, S. (1997). *The Mirror Makers: A History of American Advertising and Its Creators*. University of Illinois Press.

FTC v. Royal Milling Co. (1933). 288 U.S. 212.

Gaskill, N. B. (1936). *The Regulation of Competition*. Harper & Brothers.

Hess, H. W. (1922). History and Present Status of the 'Truth-in-Advertising' Movement as Carried on by the Vigilance Committee of the Associated Advertising Clubs of the World. *Annals of the American Academy of Political and Social Science, 101*(1), 211–220.

Kittelle, S. S., & Mastow, E. (1940). A Review of the Trade Practice Conferences of the Federal Trade Commission. *George Washington Law Review, 8*(3), 427–451.

Jacob Siegel Co. v. FTC (1946). 327 U.S. 608.

Jacobs, M. (2005). *Pocketbook Politics: Economic Citizenship in Twentieth-Century America*. Princeton University Press.

Longhurst, J. (2015). *Bike Battles: A History of Sharing the American Road*. University of Washington Press.

Masland Duraleather Co. v. FTC (1929). 34 F.2d 733 (3rd Cir.).

Mayer, R. N. (1989). *The Consumer Movement: Guardians of the Marketplace*. Twayne Publishers.

McGovern, C. (2006). *Sold American: Consumption and Citizenship 1890–1945*. University of North Carolina Press.

Mezerik, A. G. (1943, January 15). What Will Government-Imposed Standardization Mean to Advertising? *Printers' Ink, 205*, 64–67.

Newman, K. M. (2004). *Radio Active: Advertising and Consumer Activism, 1935–1947*. University of California Press.

Petty, R. D. (2011). The Co-development of Trademark Law and the Concept of Brand Marketing in the U.S. Before 1946. *Journal of Macromarketing, 31*(1), 85–99.

Petty, R. D. (2015). The Historic Development of Modern US Advertising Regulation. *Journal of Historical Research in Marketing, 7*(4), 524–548.

Petty, R. D. (2018). The US Battle against Brand Marketing: Circa 1930–1980. *Journal of Historical Research in Marketing, 10*(1), 60–85.

Richards, J. I. (2022). *A History of Advertising: The First 300,000 Years*. Bowman & Littlefield.

Ritz Distributors Corp. v. FTC (1944). 143 F.2d 676 (2nd Cir.).

Robinson, J. (1933). *The Economics of Imperfect Competition*. Macmillan

Spring, D. (2011). *Advertising in the Age of Persuasion: Building Brand America 1941–1961*. Palgrave Macmillan.

Stole, I. L. (2006). *Advertising on Trial: Consumer Activism and Corporate Public Relations in the 1930s*. University of Illinois Press.

Stole, I. L. (2012). *Advertising at War: Business Consumers and Government in the 1940s*. University of Chicago Press.

Temporary National Economic Committee. (1941). *Price Behavior and Business Policy: Monograph No. 1–3*. U.S. Government Printing Office.

Wall Street Journal. (1942, September 3). Trade-Marks Dropped in Concentration Plan for Bicycle Production. *Wall Street Journal*, 1.

Warne, C. E. (1934). Present day Advertising—The Consumer's Viewpoint. *Annals of the American Academy of Political and Social Science, 173*(May), 70–79.

Wilcox, C. (1934, May). Brand Names, Quality and Price. *Annals of the American Academy of Political and Social Science, 173*, 80–85.

Wood, J. P. (1958). *The Story of Advertising*. Ronald Press Co.

CHAPTER 10

The 1946 U.S. Lanham Act: Expanding Trademark Law

Abstract After World War II, most Americans were hungry for branded goods during this period of extended prosperity. The advertising industry participated in the propaganda support of the war that helped gain legitimacy for private brand advertising. The Lanham Act was enacted in 1946 that clarified and expanded trademark law. Marketing academics began to appreciate the significance of brand marketing that became a popular topic for academic studies. As businesses also began to appreciate the importance of brand marketing, many of them adopted the brand manager form of organization.

Keywords Lanham Act · McDonald's · Trademark licensing · Brand managers

Although consumer and labor groups favored continuing price controls under the Office of Price Administration after World War II, the agency was dissolved in mid-1946 as Republicans gained seats in the House and Senate in the election of 1946 using the slogan "Had Enough?" (Jacobs, 2005, 222–230) The National Associations of Consumers formed in 1947 to continue lobbying for consumer interests. It proposed over 100

© The Author(s), under exclusive license to Springer Nature Switzerland AG 2024
R. D. Petty, *From Marking Products to Marketing Brands*, Palgrave Studies in Marketing, Organizations and Society,
https://doi.org/10.1007/978-3-031-76778-4_10

new laws but disbanded a decade later without seeing any of them enacted (Newman, 2004, 163–164).

After World War II, war-deprived consumers were eager for branded goods and willing to pay higher prices for them. National output of goods and services doubled between 1946 and 1956 and doubled again by 1970. During this same period, private consumption accounted for two-thirds of the gross national product (Cohen, 2003, 121). Advertising expenditures increased from $2.2 billion in 1941 to $2.9 billion in 1945 (still below the $3.4 billion peak in 1929). They increased to $5.7 billion in 1950, $19.6 billion in 1970 and $54.6 billion in 1980 (Fox, 1997, 170, 172, 327). Post-war America loved business, prosperity, and brand marketing.

Economist John Kenneth Galbraith would later argue that the large increase in national demand after World War II would require businesses not only must produce more output to generate economic prosperity but also produce demand for the additional production through advertising and salesmanship. Although he did not explicitly condemn brand marketing, Galbraith (1958, 152–160) did feel that only rich consumers could afford to indulge their whims for higher priced branded goods as compared to poor consumers who had to be price sensitive to fulfill their basic needs. He also argued that affluent societies were out-of-balance producing a disproportionate amount of (branded) private goods as opposed to public goods like education or public safety services.

Despite Galbraith's opinion of poor consumers, post-war affluence seemed to quell much of the prior protest against brand marketing and stimulate the sales of branded products. As with World War I, the advertising industry participated in the war effort as the Advertising War Council and gained legitimacy for brand advertising. This legitimacy of promotion would apply to branded goods after the war (Stole, 2012).

ENTER THE LANHAM ACT

The recession and criticism of brand marketing in the 1920s and 1930s kept Congress from considering any new trademark legislation. Finally in 1938, the original Lanham Act was introduced and became the subject of congressional hearings and debates. It was not adopted until after World War II when brand marketing was welcomed by war-weary consumers. By the time the 1946 Lanham Act was enacted, some 300,000 marks had been federally registered under the prior statutes (Wilkins, 1992, 77).

A Senate committee report described trademarks as "the essence of competition" because they enabled consumers to distinguish and choose among various products. The report also enunciated the historical justifications of trademark law—to assure consumers that trademark-branded goods are genuine (not unauthorized imitations) thereby encouraging brands to invest in quality (McClure, 1979, 333–334).

The Lanham Act continued to allow, but not require, federal registration for distinctive marks already being used in interstate commerce. Trademark registrations may still last for perpetuity but must be renewed every ten years. At the initial five-year renewal, trademark registrants may seek to have their trademark declared incontestable to gain presumptions of validity as to the mark itself, the registrant's ownership in the mark, and its exclusive right to use of the mark in commerce. The renewal requirement not only creates an ongoing revenue stream for the USPTO, but allows abandoned marks to be identified, since few who abandon marks notify the USPTO requesting cancelation.

Before discussing the trademark expansions in the Lanham Act, it is important to note that the Lanham Act was not a total victory for brand marketers. The Department of Justice opposed the act arguing that trademarks in the hands of big business could be monopolistic (Rogers, 1949, 183–184). To appease Justice, the Lanham Act did not include Schechter's (1927) dilution proposal. The new act also authorized challenges to a trademark's registration (even if declared incontestable) on certain enumerated grounds: (1) the registration was obtained fraudulently; (2) the trademark has been abandoned; (3) the registration is being used to misrepresent the source of the goods or services; (4) the mark has become generic; and the mark has been used to violate the antitrust laws (McClure, 1979, 334). Note that while incontestable marks may be challenged for having become generic, they may not be challenged on the grounds of being merely descriptive (*Park 'N Fly, Inc. v. Dollar Park & Fly, Inc.*, 1985).

TRADEMARK EXPANSIONS

For the most part, courts would interpret the Lanham Act as simply adopting reforms that they had already created (McClure, 1979, 330–335). For example, prior to 1946, federal trademark law required that trademarks be "affixed" to goods or their packaging. However, there was no requirement of affixation in passing off cases involving trade names.

To address this issue the Lanham Act was expanded to cover unregistered trademark use and passing off (*Joshua Meier Co. v. Albany Novelty Manufacturing Co.*, 1956). It also replaced the affixation requirement with the requirement that trademarks be used in connection with the sale of goods or services (Barrett, 2006, 380–383). This set up the statute to also authorize marks for service brands which it did. The Lanham Act also authorized collective and certification marks. Reminiscent of guild marks, collective marks are used by members of the mark-owning organization and certification marks are used by those who satisfy standards of a certifying organization (Petty, 2016, 144).

Infringement also was expanded first by expansive Lanham Act language that infringement would cover not just confusion about source but also include likely confusion of source, sponsorship, or endorsement. In addition, a 1962 statutory amendment eliminated the need to prove likely confusion by purchasers. As a result, some courts recognized post-purchase or onlooker confusion (*Mastercrafters Clock & Radio Co. v. Vacheron & Constantin-LeCoultre Watches, Ltd.*, 1955), and initial interest confusion by potential purchasers even if the confusion was corrected before purchase or no purchase was made (*Grotrian, Helfferich, Schultz, Th. Steinweg Nachf. v. Steinway & Sons*, 1975). Both types of confusion, although not yet widely adopted, provide further brand protection in cases where purchasers are not ultimately confused as to the brand identity.

TRADEMARK LICENSING TO THIRD PARTIES

The Lanham Act clarified trademark law by requiring trademark sales be registered with the Patent and Trademark Office and be accompanied by the sale of assets needed to manufacture the trademarked goods. This practice allowed (but did not require) manufacturing to continue at the same level of quality that consumers come to associate with the mark. A mere license of the trademark to a third party on the other hand only requires that the registrant be able to exercise quality control over the licensee's product. The clarification of trademark licensing and sale rules probably encouraged licensing.

Trademark licensing started before the Lanham Act in the 1930s with Shirley Temple dolls and Mickey Mouse merchandise, but it did not take off until the 1950s after clarification by the Lanham Act. By the early 1980s, retail sales of toys and other merchandise of Star Wars licensed merchandise exceeded $1.5 billion (Battersby & Grimes, 1986, 273). The licensing of sports team merchandise also was stimulated by the Lanham Act. The new language that infringement includes likely confusion of source, sponsorship, or endorsement could be applied against unlicensed merchandise vendors. By 1982 most courts had decided trademark owners needed some evidence of confusion regarding source, sponsorship, or endorsement regarding unlicensed merchandise sellers (*National Football League Properties, Inc. v. Wichita Falls Sportswear, Inc.*, 1982). Such evidence was not difficult to obtain from appropriate consumer surveys (Dogan & Lemley, 2005).

Allowing trademark licensing with quality control also provided the legal basis for modern business method franchising as used by McDonald's and many other firms. The franchisor develops its trademarked brand identity and a business format that provides for quality control and licenses both to franchisees. This saves the franchisor from the expense of owning all of its own retail outlets and allows franchisees to reduce risk by investing in a proven brand and business format rather than trying to develop their own brand and format.

Fast food and other roadside services were stimulated to franchise with the growth of the interstate highway system in the 1950s. In 1950, only about 100 companies offered business format franchises. That number grew to about 900 in 1960 with an estimated 200,000 outlets. By the late 1960s, McDonald's, Holiday Inn, and KFC were all close to having one thousand units or more. Between 1964 and 1969, an estimated 100,000 new franchise businesses began (Herman, 2003).

RESTRICTING TRADEMARK USE BY NON-COMPETITORS

The Lanham Act did not include Schechter's (1927) concept of trademark dilution from trademark use by non-competing products. However, courts stepped in to recognize that the question of whether the imitator was in the same industry as the trademark registrant was not a simple yes or no question. In many disputes, the industries are somewhat similar. To analyze the degree of similarity, courts developed a multi-factor method of analysis did not develop a consistent method of analysis for cross-product infringement that was first proposed in the 1938 Restatement of Torts. The Second Circuit Court of Appeals was the first court to adopt a list of factors (*Polaroid Corp. v. Polarad Electronics, Corp.*, 1961):

- Strength of the first (senior) user's mark.
- Similarity (appearance, sound, etc.) of the marks.
- Proximity of goods & Likelihood of brand extension.
- New (junior) user's intent.
- Evidence of actual confusion.
- Care of buyers.
- Quality of junior user's goods—courts disagree on whether a significant disparity in quality between the senior and junior user's goods make harm from confusion more likely or make the probability of confusion less likely.

By explicitly examining the proximity of goods and often similarity of channels of distribution, courts acknowledge that trademark use on non-competing goods, particularly if somewhat related to the type of goods that originally used the trademark, could be challenged for confusing consumers about the source of the products. But courts tempered this expansion by also examining the sophistication of consumers and looking for evidence of actual confusion or intent to confuse. The Second Circuit's *Polaroid* factors would soon be imitated with some variation by the other Circuits. They allowed courts to condemn some uses of trademarks on non-competing goods, but not all such uses.

Brand Marketing Literature

The post-World War II liberalization of U.S. trademark law coincided with a dramatic increase in the brand marketing literature. A seminal *Journal of Marketing* article on brand extensions by Aaker and Keller (1990) is often suggested as the start of this literature (e.g., Moor, 2007, 3). However, this modern phase appears to be a third phase of brand marketing literature. Aaker and Keller (1990) no more started the literature on brand marketing then they started the discussion of brand extensions, which dates back much earlier (e.g., Printers' Ink, 1922).

Phase one of the literature, e.g., trademark advertising, was examined in Chapter 7. Schwarzkopf (2010, 168) notes there also was literature on brand marketing from the mid-1950s to the mid-1970s. He posits that this literature was the explicit codification of knowledge that had previously been developed as implicit knowledge within advertising agency practice in the early twentieth century. This literature also may be based on the trademark advertising literature of phase one.

Phase two arguably begins with "Techniques of Appraising Brand Preference and Brand Consciousness by Consumer Interviewing" in the *Journal of Marketing* (Wolfe, 1942), the post-World War II literature starts with Gardner and Levy's (1955), discussion the difference between the product and the brand in the *Harvard Business Review*. They recognized the 'brand name' (rather than trademark) as a complex symbol representing a variety of ideas and attributes that build up in the minds of consumers over time. The net result was a brand personality that might be more important for sales than technical aspects of the product (Gardner & Levy, 1955, 35; Levy, 1959). This article created a "sensation in the business world" (Bastos & Levy, 2012, 355–356) and was the inspiration for adman David Ogilvy's emphasis on brand image and brand personality (Schwarzkopf, 2010, 188). Ogilvy also was influenced by Claude Hopkins, 1923 book, *Scientific Advertising* (Schwarzkopf, 2009).

The Gardner and Levy (1955) conceptual article was quickly followed by an empirical study of the importance of the brand in making continuing sales. Cunningham (1956) reported on the results of a three-year consumer panel study of brand loyalty. He found that many purchasers were loyal to at least some brands with some being secondarily loyal to a second brand. However, brand loyalty varied across consumers and product categories. There did not seem to be any 'loyalty-prone' consumers who were loyal to a brand in every category of low-priced frequently purchased products in the study. These studies may have led the Oxford English Dictionary to disdainfully recognize "brand image" in 1959 (Bastos & Levy, 2012).

Although not always explicitly evoking the term "brand marketing," the literature on that topic continued. In 1960, Theodore Levitt cautioned marketers not to define their business too narrowly as the railroads had done. Instead, he urged that the business firm think of itself not as producing products, but rather as "buying customers, as doing the things that will make people want to do business with it" (Levitt, 1960, 12). This early post-World War II literature is consistent with Morein (1975) noting that the previous twenty-five years had seen the development of sophisticated brand marketing for consumer products.

In 1964, Tucker (1964) presented his study on the development of brand loyalty. Other studies were showing that customers often preferred families of brands—brands that were used for two or more similar products such as fruits and vegetables or various paper products (Fry, 1967). At this point, lawyers were writing articles for marketing managers on the importance of protecting trademarks of brand names (e.g., Diamond, 1962).

Edward Tauber (1981) later built upon Levitt (1960) by suggesting that existing brand names could be used not only for line extensions of similar products but also for new product categories. Both Tauber (1981, 39) and Ries and Trout (1981) recognized the risks of such strategies and the fact that the new opportunity had to be appropriate for the brand. The latter book, *Positioning: The Battle for Your Mind*, is a modern classic on the concept of brand marketing, even though 'brand' does not appear in the title nor very often in the text. Finally, no review of the pre-1990 branding literature would be complete without reference to Dorothy Cohen's (1986) article where she urged marketers to take a strategic approach to trademark strategy by learning about trademark law and administration as well as conducting surveys and behavioral studies to support their firm's trademarks.

Brand Managers

The growing brand marketing literature and the post-World War II expansion of brand protection added to duties to those who managed brands. They now had to consider developing new types of brand identifiers as registered trademarks, enforcement against similar but not identical marks beyond immediate competitors, possible licensing and brand extension opportunities, and renewal of active trademarks every ten years. With this proliferation of brand management duties and a proliferation of the number of brands at many companies, functional managers such as a manager of advertising could be easily overwhelmed. For this reason, many firms shifted to a brand management form of organization.

As Low and Fullerton (1994), document the concept of product or brand managers originated in 1930 but did not take off until after World War II. They report that by 1967 most large consumer packaged goods companies had brand managers. During this time, most advertising agencies gave up their role as "counselors and almost-equal partners in brand management" to focus on media and creative work (Low & Fullerton, 1994, 182).

CASE STUDY: MCDONALD'S FAMILY OF BRANDS

The first McDonald's drive-in restaurant was opened in 1940 by hot dog stand operators Maurice ("Mac") and Richard McDonald in San Bernardino, California. The brothers developed a self-service counter that eliminated the need for waiters and waitresses. By 1949, the menu was condensed to include 15-cent hamburgers, shakes, and fries. Customers received their food quickly because hamburgers were pre-cooked and warmed under heat lamps.

McDonald's was a huge success, and the brothers began a franchise program of ten additional restaurants. Ray Kroc, who sold Multimixer milkshake machines, visited the brothers in 1954. The following year he became their franchise agent and opened the first McDonald's east of the Mississippi river. In 1960, the company's gross sales were $56 million from its 228 restaurants. The following year Kroc bought the rights to the brothers' company for $2.7 million and in 1965, Kroc took the company public. By 1970, McDonald's had 1500 restaurants that grew to 6200 in 1980 (Encyclopedia Britanica, 2024).

In January 1963, McDonald's registered its name as a federal trademark claiming first use in December 1948 and first use in interstate commerce in May 1953. Its "arches" trademark also was registered in 1963 with a first use in 1961. McDonald's next extended its trademark strategy to individual menu items including the Big Mac in 1979 (claiming first use in 1957) and the Egg McMuffin in 1973 as a stylized mark and 1975 as a word mark (claiming first use in 1972 both).

Meanwhile, during the 1960s, courts and the trademark office developed the legal concept of a family of trademarks (*Maidenform, Inc. v. Bestform Foundations, Inc.*, 1969; *Motorola Inc. v. Griffiths Electrons, Inc.*, 1963; Petty, 2010). Marks constituting a family are registered by one company and contain a recognizable characteristic in common. If advertised and promoted together, the family is thought to have broader protection over a single mark against similar marks used by other parties. For McDonald's the common characteristic is "Mc-" " or "Mac-" connected to a generic food name (Petty, 2016, 68–74).

In the first litigated case involving McDonald's family of trademarks, the court noted that McDonald's had a dozen "Mc-" trademarks and ran advertising in 1976 using commonplace words added to the "Mc-" prefix such as McFriendliest and McGreatest. The court further recognized a lengthy record of judgments, consent decrees, and agreements preventing competitors from using the "Mc-" prefix. The court enjoined McBagels from using that name or any other "Mc-" plus generic food-name combination (*McDonald's Corp. v. McBagels, Inc.*, 1986).

A court decision nine years later noted McDonald's then had a total of 51 registered trademarks and service marks of the "Mc-" or "Mac-" variety. It then provided more specific information:

> marks used by opposer [i.e. McDonald's] for food services or for food products include "Chicken McNuggets"; "McPizza"; "Mayor McCheeze"; "Egg McMuffin"; "McBoo"; "McChili"; "McFax"; "McBagel"; "McHappy"; "Chicken McSwiss"; "McRib"; "McChicken"; "Mc D.L.T."; "McDinner"; "McDonuts"; "McPack"; "McSnack"; and "McStop." Other members of the family, used on and registered for goods and services which are not necessarily related to restaurant services, include "McClip" for hair-cutting services; "McClass" for computer services; "McCash" for financial services; "McD" for cleaning products; "McBucks" for redeemable certificates; "McBunny" for toys; "McMatch" for games; "McShirt" for clothing; "McGift Shop" for retail store services; "McHat" for hats; "McLots of Fun" for stage productions; "McMasters" for recruiting elderly employees; "McShuttle" for transportation services; "McBear" for stuffed toys; "McKids" for children's clothing sold at Sears retail stores; and "McJobs" for training handicapped people. Many of these marks are used through licensing programs opposer has with other businesses. (*McDonald's Corp. v. John L. McClain*, 1995)

In this second decision, the Trademark Trial and Appeal Board affirmed the trademark office's denied registration of "McClaim's" for legal services (also using the slogan "Fast Food Justice"). The Board conceded that consumers would not confuse a restaurant with a law office but given McDonald's extensive licensing program outside of food service, customers are likely to falsely believe the law office is licensed or otherwise connected to McDonald's in some way (*McDonald's Corp. v. John L. McClain*, 1995) (Fig. 10.1).

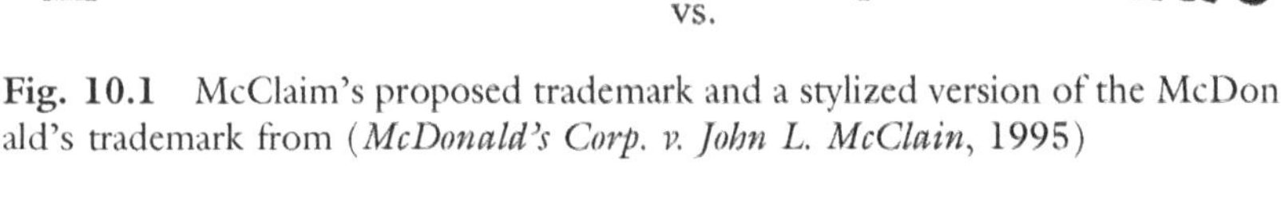

Fig. 10.1   McClaim's proposed trademark and a stylized version of the McDonald's trademark from (*McDonald's Corp. v. John L. McClain*, 1995)

This broad interpretation of the scope of McDonald's family of trademarks was supported by two earlier cases. In 1988 McDonald's won a case involving a proposed trademark for a budget hotel—McSleep Inn. The court noted that restaurants are often associated with specific hotels (*Quality Inns International, Inc. v. McDonald's Corp.*, 1988). Five years later, it obtained a permanent injunction of a dentist office from using the name McDental. The court conducted a complete analysis of the likelihood of confusion factors finding confusion about a connection was likely (*McDonald's Corp. v. Druck and Gerner, DDS, PC.*, 1993).

Most of McDonald's trademark challenges involve food and some of its cease-and-desist letters to similar "McTrademarks." More formal disputes are listed in the table below. Those challenges are generally successful in the U.S., but results in other countries are mixed (Leong & Lwin, 2006) (Table 10.1).

The list above suggests McDonald's spends significant resources monitoring trademark applications and use throughout the world. Yet McDonald's undoubtedly contacts many more brand marketers with "Mc-" trademarks. Occasionally such "cease and desist" letters are reported in the press (David Bollier, 2005, 6, 212). McDonald's also is ready to take formal action if necessary. For example, the U.S. trademark office lists 25 oppositions to proposed "Mc-" trademarks from 1986 to the present. Eleven of its oppositions terminated trademark applications in 2024.

It is not clear whether McDonald's started its family of names as its own marketing idea or whether publicly created nicknames such as McDonut and McPizza inspired the tactic. In either case, while McDonald's did not invent the family of brands concept, it has brought more enforcement actions based on this concept than any other brand marketer.

Table 10.1 Legal challenges by McDonald's of "Mc-"Names—updated from (Petty, 2016, 71)

Name	Year	Location	Allowed	Comments
Its not just big, Mac	1985	UK	No	Slogan used by rival Burger King; Did not imply Big Mac had less beef
McBagels	1986	US	No	Food
McSleep Inns	1988	US	No	Hotels often related to restaurants
McTeddy (Bears)	1990	US	No	McDonald's features toys in kid's meals
McPretzel	1991	US	No	Food
McDental	1993	US	No	Likely consumer confusion (?)
McBeans	1994	Canada	Yes	Coffee sold in stores not restaurant
McHair	1995	Austria	Yes	Hairdressing services & products distinct from fast food
McAllan	1995	Denmark	No	Used by hot dog stand
McClaim's Legal Services	1995	US	No	Likely consumer confusion (?)
McIndians	1996	UK	No	Indian restaurant also sold fried chicken, burgers & fries
McSalad, McFresh	1997	Australia	No	Deceptively similar
McMint and McVeg	1997	Australia	Yes	Confectionary business distinct; McVeg for a veggie hamburger confusion unlikely!!
McChina Wok Away	2001	UK	Yes	McD's doesn't serve Chinese food and the name means "son of China"
MacChocolate, MacTea, MacNoodles	2004	Singapore	Yes	Sold through supermarkets using dissimilar mark design
Big Mak hamburgers	2004	Philippines	No	Ordered to also pay damages
McVeggie	2005	Argentina	No	
McCurry	2006	Malaysia	No	Colors also similar
MACDIMSUM	2013	UK	No	
McSweet	2014	US	No	Likely infringement & dilution

(continued)

Table 10.1 (continued)

Name	Year	Location	Allowed	Comments
McCoffee	2016	EU	No	For food & beverages
McVegan	2022	UK	No	Bad faith found
Supermac	2024	Ireland, EU	Yes	Allowed as restaurant name but not name of beef products. Big Mac delisted as McDonald's trademark for restaurant & poultry products but not hamburgers

REFERENCES

Aaker, D. A., & Keller, K. L. (1990). Consumer Evaluations of Brand Extensions. *Journal of Marketing, 54*(1), 27–41.

Barrett, M. (2006). Internet Trademark Suits and the Demise of "Trademark Use". *U.C. Davis Law Review, 39*(2), 371.

Bastos, W. & Levy, S.J. (2012). A History of the Concept of Branding: Practice and Theory. *Journal of Historical Research in Marketing, 14*(3), 347–368.

Battersby, G. J., & Grimes, C. W. (1986). Merchandise Revisited. *The Trademark Reporter, 76*(4), 271–307.

Bollier, D. (2005). *Brand Names Bullies: The Quest to Own and Control Culture.* Wiley.

Britanica Money. (2024). *McDonald's.* https://www.britannica.com/money/McDonalds

Cohen, D. (1986). Trademark Strategy. *Journal of Marketing, 50*(1), 61–74.

Cohen, L. (2003). *A Consumers' Republic: The Politics of Mass Consumption in Postwar America.* Knopf.

Cunningham, R. M. (1956). Brand loyalty—What, where how much? *Harvard Business Review 34,*116–28.

Diamond, S. A. (1962). Protect Your Trademark by Proper Usage. *Journal of Marketing, 26*(3), 17–22. https://doi.org/10.1177/002224296202600303

Dogan, S. L., & Lemley, M. A. (2005). The Merchandising Right: Fragile Theory or Fait Accompli? *Emory Law Journal, 54*(Winter), 461–506.

Fox, S. (1997). *The Mirror Makers: A History of American Advertising and Its Creators.* University of Illinois Press.

Fry, J. N. (1967). Family Branding and Consumer Brand Choice. *Journal of Marketing Research, 4*(3), 237–247.

Galbraith, J. K. (1958). *The Affluent Society.* Houghton Mifflin Harcourt.

Gardner, B. B., & Levy, S. J. (1955). The Product and the Brand. *Harvard Business Review, 33*(2), 33–39.

Herman, M. L. (2003.). *A Brief History of Franchising.* https://www.intern ationalfranchiselaw.com/franchise-law-overview/about-franchising/a-brief-his tory-of-franchising

Hopkins, C. C. (1923). *Scientific Advertising.* Lord and Thomas.

Jacobs, M. (2005). *Pocketbook Politics: Economic Citizenship in Twentieth-Century America.* Princeton University Press.

Joshua Meier Co. v. Albany Novelty Manufacturing Co. (1956). 236 F.2d 144 (2d Cir.).

Leong, S., & Lwin, M. O. (2006). Marketing and the Law: Seeking Exclusivity over a Brand Naming System? The McDonald's Experience. *Journal of the Academy of Marketing Science, 34*(1), 84–85. https://doi.org/10.1177/009 2070305283686

Levitt, T. (1960, July/August). Marketing Myopia. *Harvard Business Review, 38,* 45–56.

Levy, S. J. (1959). Symbols for Sale. *Harvard Business Review, 37*(4), 117–124.

Long, C. (2006). Dilution. *Columbia Law Review, 106*(June), 1029–1076.

Low, G., & Fullerton, R. (1994). Brands, Brand Management, and the Brand Manager System: A Critical-Historical Evaluation. *Journal of Marketing Research, 31*(2), 173–190.

Maidenform, Inc. v. Bestform Foundations, Inc. (1969). 161 U.S.P.Q. 805 (T.T.A.B.).

Mastercrafters Clock & Radio Co. v. Vacheron & Constantin-Le Coultre Watches, Inc. (1955). 221 F.2d 464 (2d Cir).

McClure, D. M. (1979, July–August). Trademarks and Unfair Competition: A Critical History of Legal Thought. *Trademark Reporter, 69,* 305–356.

McDonald's Corp. v. Druck and Gerner, DDS, PC. (1993) 814 F. Supp. 1127 (N.D.N.Y).

McDonald's Corp. v. McBagels, Inc. (1986). 649 F. Supp 1268 (S.D.N.Y.).

McDonald's Corp. v. McClain. (1995). 37 U.S.P.Q.2d 1274 (TTAB).

Moor, L. (2007). *The Rise of Brands.* Berg.

Morein, J. A. (1975). Shift from Brand to Product Line Marketing. *Harvard Business Review, 53*(5), 56–64.

Moseley v. V. Secret Catalogue, Inc. (2003). 537 U.S. 418.

Motorola Inc. v. Griffiths Electrons, Inc. (1963), 317 F.2d 397 (C.C.P.A.).

National Football League v. Wichita Falls Sportswear. (1982). 532 F. Supp. 651 (W.D. Wash.).

Newman, K. M. (2004). *Radio Active: Advertising and Consumer Activism, 1935–1947.* University of California Press.

Park 'N Fly, Inc. v. Dollar Park & Fly, Inc. (1985). 469 U.S. 189.

Petty, R. D. (2010). Naming Names: Part three—Safeguarding Brand Equity in the United States by Developing a Family of Trademarks. *Journal of Brand Management, 17*(8), 561–567.

Petty, R. D. (2016), *Branding Law: A Guide to the Legal Issues in Brand Management*. West Academic.

Polaroid Corporation v. Polarad Electronics Corp. (1961). 287 F. 2d 492 (2d Cir.).

Printers' Ink. (1922). Slogans No Longer Registerable. *Printers' Ink, 121*(4), 53–55.

Ries, A., & Trout, J. (1981). *Positioning: The Battle for Your Mind*. McGraw Hill.

Rogers, E. S. (1949). The Lanham Act and the Social Function of Trade-Marks. *Law and Contemporary Problems, 14*(Spring), 173–184.

Quality Inns International, Inc. v. McDonald's Corp. (1988). 695 F. Supp. 198 (D. Md.).

Schechter, F. I. (1927). The Rational Basis of Trademark Protection. *Harvard Law Review, 40*(6), 813–833.

Schwarzkopf, S. (2009). What was advertising? The invention, rise, demise, and disappearance of advertising concepts in nineteenth- and twentieth-century Europe and America. In *Business and Economic History Online, 7*, 1–27. https://thebhc.org/sites/default/files/schwarzkopf.pdf.

Schwarzkopf, S. (2010). Turning Trademarks into Brands: How Advertising Agencies Practiced and Conceptualized Branding, 1890–1930. In T. da Silva Lopes & P. Duguid (Eds.), *Trademarks, Brands, and Competitiveness* (pp. 165–193). Routledge.

Stole, I. L. (2012). *Advertising at War: Business Consumers and Government in the 1940s*. University of Chicago Press.

Tauber, E. M. (1981). Brand Franchise Extension: New Product Benefits from Existing Brand Names. *Business Horizons, 24*(2), 36–41.

Tucker, W. T. (1964). The Development of Brand Loyalty. *Journal of Marketing Research, 1*(3), 32–35.

Wilkins, M. (1992). The Neglected Intangible Asset: The Influence of the Trade Mark on the Rise of the Modern Corporation. *Business History, 34*(1), 66–95.

Wolfe, H. D. (1942). Techniques of Appraising Brand Preference and Brand Consciousness by Consumer Interviewing. *Journal of Marketing, 6*(4), 81–87.

CHAPTER 11

Challenges to Brand Marketing 1946–1980

Abstract Academic debate over brand marketing continued after World War II influencing the Federal Trade Commission to take action. The FTC challenged a couple of market-dominating trademarks and accused the leading breakfast cereals of sharing a monopoly. It also pursued mergers between two strong brands that would increase the brands' position in the market. Additionally, the FTC also accused ReaLemon of monopolizing the market for reconstituted lemon juice. Lastly, the Commission developed several information disclosure programs to refocus consumers on information over brand with several programs to encourage energy conservation.

Keywords Brand criticism · ReaLemon brand · Federal Trade Commission · Information disclosure · Antitrust · Mergers · Market-dominating brands · Borden Co

Despite post-war America's embrace of brand marketing occasional popular books peripherally criticized it. In addition to John Kenneth Galbraith's *The Affluent Society* (1958) discussed in the last chapter, Vance Packard wrote *The Hidden Persuaders* criticizing various persuasive advertising techniques. In passing, Packard (1958, 16–17) argued that

© The Author(s), under exclusive license to Springer Nature Switzerland AG 2024
R. D. Petty, *From Marking Products to Marketing Brands*, Palgrave Studies in Marketing, Organizations and Society,
https://doi.org/10.1007/978-3-031-76778-4_11

one reason why advertisers were forced to develop such techniques was the increased standardization of products. These similar products were then sold by persuading consumers that there were differences between brands when there really were not. He quotes ad agency president David Ogilvy: "The greater the similarity between products, the less part reason really plays in brand selection." Although popular, these books failed to arouse a popular consumer movement to oppose some aspects of brand marketing the way Chase and Schlink (1927) did thirty years earlier.

Similarly, despite the Department of Justice's initial opposition to what would become the Lanham Act, it and other antitrust authorities appear to have lost interest in the monopolistic aspects of brand marketing after World War II. Congressional antitrust hearings instead criticized increasing industrial concentration and administered (coordinated) pricing thought to contribute to inflation (Williamson, 1995, 46).

Even the Attorney General's antitrust review committee supported the use of trademarks except where trademark licensing involved an unreasonable restraint of trade such as division of markets among competitors (Barnes & Oppenheim, 1955, 87). A majority of the committee also opposed legislation authorizing resale price maintenance by brands with their retailers and favored ignoring branding differences when determining whether two products were of "like grade and quality" for price discrimination purposes (Barnes & Oppenheim, 1955, 153–154, 157).

While antitrust authorities appear uninterested in challenging brand marketing other than price discrimination, courts in the 1940s and early 1950s continued occasional denouncements of trademark monopolies in trademark cases (Pattishall, 1952, 973–977). Ultimately by the 1980s, courts would come to accept brand marketing and the importance of trademarks thereto (McClure, 1996, 33–34).

ACADEMIC CRITICISM

The lack of a public reform movement after World War II did not mean brand marketing was not criticized. To the contrary, the criticism continued, largely out of the public eye, within antitrust scholarship and regulatory agencies. Critics still condemned brand marketing for limiting competition between similar brands in part by causing higher advertising expenses. Products that were promoted more by brand rather than product attributes or performance also were criticized for failing to provide consumers with information about product attributes or performance (Petty, 2018).

For example, in 1948 Yale Law School professor Ralph Brown continued brand marketing criticism with his now classic article "Advertising and the Public Interest: Legal Protection of Trade Symbols." In this article he argues that contrary to the belief of many economists that advertising's purpose is to provide information to consumers, that "[m]ost advertising, however, is designed not to inform, but to persuade and influence" (Brown, 1948, 1169).

Brown essentially argues that advertising manipulates and persuades consumers to consistently buy particular brands which, enabled by trademark protection, creates monopolistic competition where brand marketers are able to charge higher prices because they are insulated to some degree from competition by similar products. However, Brown appears to concede the entrenchment of brand marketing calling only for the narrow enforcement of trademark infringement law while otherwise allowing firms to compete using somewhat similar trade symbols and persuasive advertising.

Two years later economist Nicholas Kaldor (1950) agreed that most advertising was persuasive and that the funds being expended on advertising were not justifiable solely to communicate information. He recognized that brand marketing efforts likely increased industrial concentration but that in turn might lead to economies of scale, but he was skeptical whether such economies would justify the large amounts spent on advertising.

Kaldor's (1950) theoretical exposition was followed by Bain's (1956) empirical examination of 20 manufacturing industries patterned after Borden's (1942) study. Like the earlier TNEC report, Bain (1956) found product differentiation to be unimportant in some industries such as rayon and cement but of great significance in others such as liquor, cigarettes, and automobiles. He argued that both product design and brand differentiation supported by substantial advertising and promotion efforts can create a preference for those goods in the minds of consumers leading to an advantage over new entrants. This differentiation advantage allowed existing firms to raise prices compared to competing products and not lose substantial sales. Moreover, this advantage forced new entrants to offer a lower price or incur higher selling costs to successfully enter (Bain, 1956, 113–117).

Bain (1956, 216–217) was reluctant to develop policy recommendations concluding that human nature was the root of the problem. Nevertheless, he vaguely suggested that policies to encourage information dissemination such as comprehensive grade labeling and restricting marketing expenditures might be beneficial.

Next "Chicago School" economists entered the discussion of brand advertising and competition, disputing the prior view that advertising is "persuasive" and arguing instead that advertising is informative and reduces consumer's search costs (Stigler, 1961). Telser (1964) conceded that some advertising might be persuasive and lead to monopoly power but also argued that advertising was essential for new entrants and therefore could be pro-competitive. He then examined advertising intensity (advertising/sales) and found a weak ("unimpressive") positive correlation with four firm concentration level and an inverse relationship with market share stability suggesting advertising was largely pro-competitive.

Comanor and Wilson (1967, 1974) offered additional theoretical and empirical support for the view that brand advertising was anticompetitive. They found that advertising intensity was correlated with profit rates and in some industries advertising expenditures act as an important barrier to entry to new competition. At this point, as the scholarship debate continued, the FTC began several antitrust-based actions challenging the conduct of successful market-dominating brands. This was toward the end of a period of antitrust expansion that began in the 1940s and would end in the late 1970s (Petty, 2016, 267–270).

This brand marketing criticism flowed into two categories of regulatory action (Petty, 2018). First, a consumer protection initiative sought to provide accurate information to consumers to enable them to make better-informed decisions. Product names should be accurate and non-misleading and that the common name of the product be accurately disclosed. In some industries regulators also have sought to require disclosure of information about product performance so that consumers can accurately compare the performance of various brands. It is important to note that except for a couple early 1970s FTC cases and corresponding academic discussion, emotional appeals in advertising avoided scrutiny (Richards & Petty, 2007, 392–393). The second category of criticism focused on the FTC attempting to address both brand-enhancing mergers and anticompetitive brand marketing activities of market-dominating firms. Each of these two programs is discussed in turn.

ACCURATE INFORMATION DISCLOSURE

Bain (1956) echoed long-standing concerns that brand marketing emphasizes brand appeal over product information so that consumers don't have the information they need to tell whether various branded products are similar or different. The FDA and FTC developed information disclosure initiatives in the five "F" industries: food, fine jewelry, fabrics, furs, and pharmaceuticals (Petty, 2018). As discussed previously, prior to World War II, the FDA had been attempting to address this problem for foods since 1906 and the FTC since at least 1918 when it worked with members of the fine jewelry industry to develop a standardized method of disclosing the amount of gold in rings.

The FTC long pursued misleading product names in the fur and fabric industries where numerous trade or brand names falsely suggested apparel was made entirely or mostly of expensive materials such as wool, silk, mink, or leather. The FTC sought to enjoin the further inaccurate use of particular names, but new names were always being developed. Therefore, Congress enacted statutes in 1951 and 1958 authorizing the FTC to promulgate industry wide rules requiring the (generic) English language name of furs and the generic fiber name be disclosed with equal size and prominence with any trademark used in labeling or advertising of textile or fur products (Ball, 1978, 472).

A 1962 amendment to the Federal Food, Drug and Cosmetic Act imposed a similar requirement that all labels and advertising for prescription drugs contain the generic product name in type at least half as large as that used for any trade or brand name. The FTC staff conducted a twenty-year study of two drugs concluding in 1977 that the use of trademarks in these two industries had stifled competition and caused the public to pay an unnecessary price premium for the branded drugs. The pharmaceutical industry responded that generic versions of branded drugs may perform differently since they may contain differing inactive ingredients that could affect bioavailability of the active ingredient.

Ultimately, the Department of Health, Education, and Welfare passed regulations capping Medicare and Medicaid pharmaceutical reimbursement amounts to the lowest priced "chemically-equivalent" drugs. States began to replace anti-drug substitution laws with laws encouraging the substitution of lower priced generic drugs unless the prescribing physician expressly indicates the prescription should be filled "as written." By

1978, thirty-six states had adopted such pro-substitution laws (Ball, 1978, 472–484).

One final industry where the accurate identification of the product according to its ingredients has been an issue is the food industry. The FDA continued to promulgate standards of identity particularly for post-World War II refrigerated and frozen foods as well as other processed foods. The goal was to prevent food brand marketers from deceptively and falsely suggesting their products were a certain type of food in cases where the required listing of ingredients was believed insufficient to address this problem.

By 1954, such standardized foods accounted for more than half of all food purchases by American consumers. In 1961, the FDA started what turned out to be a decade long process of defining the standard of identity for peanut butter to require not less than 90% peanuts and no more than 55% fat (Food and Drug Administration 2018). Any product with a lower proportion could not identify itself as peanut butter and gain the favorable association that many consumers have with that product name (Chen, 1992). The FDA had promulgated identity standards for nearly 250 foods by 1973 (Merrill & Collier, 1974).

Requiring Useful Information Disclosure

While the FDA focused its post-war efforts on defining standard foods by ingredients, in the early 1970s the FTC focused more on disclosure of non-misleading product performance information. Brands had long been criticized for seeking to differentiate themselves from other brands through vague suggestion rather than factual information. Performance information would better allow consumers to evaluate products by performance rather than simply relying on well-known brand names hoping for good performance. Requiring information disclosure might also encourage some brands to promote their performance in advertising.

Some rules such as the Fuel Economy Guide, the Octane Rating Rule, the Home Appliance Energy Labeling Rule and the R-Value Rule (for home insulation). These rules and guides all require disclosure of specific information about energy efficiency that was not generally or uniformly disclosed in brand promotion advertising or product labeling. An FTC staff report suggests the Commission's interest in comparative performance information was a natural adjunct to its encouragement of comparative advertising that began in the early 1970s (Federal Trade

Commission, 1981, 7). But as discussed previously, at least some of the FTC information provision programs (e.g., jewelry, textiles including requiring care labeling) predate its interest in promoting comparative advertising.

The FTC staff also considered performance disclosures outside of energy to provide comparative performance information of the sort provided by *Consumer Reports* and advocated by Chase and Schlink (1927). It evaluated the feasibility of providing comparative performance information for several products including vacuum cleaners, carpets, washing machines, refrigerators, air conditioners, and dehumidifiers. However, developing such programs turned out to be more complex than anticipated, presenting both technical testing issues as well as behavioral and disclosure issues (Federal Trade Commission, 1981, 49–50). Most were abandoned.

BRAND ENHANCING MERGERS

While the FTC's consumer protection bureau was busy with information disclosure, its competition bureau pursued antitrust issues involving brand marketing. The FTC's first efforts to identify and restrict anticompetitive brand marketing involved challenging mergers that would lead to additional marketing advantages for brands that were already market dominant. This approach had the advantage of challenging the merger rather than the brand marketing itself so that the remedy would likely be divestiture rather than attempting to restrict brand marketing practices.

The FTC's first such merger case successfully challenged Proctor & Gamble's 1957 acquisition of Clorox bleach. The Commission found that all liquid bleach products were homogenous so ideally from the consumer perspective, price should drive product preferences. However, even before the merger, Clorox advertised extensively. This advertising led to more brand than price competition that would favor Clorox even more with access to P&G's advertising discounts and financial resources. The merger also eliminated P&G as a potential new entrant into the household liquid bleach market.

Within four years of the merger Clorox's market share increased from 49 to 52%. The Supreme Court agreed the merger was anticompetitive and affirmed the FTC's order of divestiture that occurred in 1969. Justice Harlan in a concurring opinion criticized the majority opinion for characterizing advertising solely as a means of market entrenchment with no benefit to consumers. He argued that advertising was informative and branding may be an assurance of quality but he agreed the merger would likely raise barriers to entry and increase prices (Ball, 1978, 493–494; *FTC v. Proctor & Gamble Co.*, 1967).

A similar FTC challenge was made to the merger of General Foods and the SOS brand of steel wool. Although General Foods was not a potential market entrant in steel wool, acquiring one of the top two steel wool brands allowed it to apply its large marketer advantages to the already dominant SOS brand. As the marketer of a large number of well-known consumer brands, General Foods enjoyed strong channel relationships and advertising discounts. A few years after the merger, SOS increased its market share of the household steel wool market from 49.6% in 1959 to 56% in 1962 while archrival Brillo's sales declined during the same period of overall market expansion. The FTC held that General Foods' acquisition of SOS and its application of promotional advantages to SOS were anticompetitive. The FTC order for General Foods to divest SOS assets was later affirmed by a court of appeals (*General Foods Corp. v. FTC*, 1967).

These two merger decisions were later limited to some degree when the FTC refused to condemn a merger in the wine industry because of the large variety of products and price points that would make any advertising advantage from the merger less effective across the entire industry. In this type of market, advertising would encourage competition by informing consumers about the variety of alternatives (*Heublein, Inc.*, 1980).

Brand Exclusion Activities

A 1969 American Bar Association report accused the FTC of focusing on unimportant cases so the new chairperson (the primary author of the ABA report) was appointed. He persuaded a Commission majority to issue a complaint in 1972 against the four largest ready-to-eat cereal companies Kellogg, General Mills, General Foods (Post), and Quaker Oats alleging they "shared" a monopoly by following each other's tactics such as price increases without any explicit collusion. The breakfast cereal industry was just the sort that Comanor and Wilson (1967, 1974) found to be anticompetitive.

The complaint accused the four firms of maintaining a shared monopoly (together they controlled about 90% of the market) by proliferating brands that artificially differentiated similar products, promoting these brands through intensive advertising, and refusing to sell private labels brands to retailers. This conduct allegedly made it difficult for new firms to enter the ready-to-eat cereal market and led to high profits for the four firms. Possible remedies could have included divesting assets to create several new independent cereal companies and compulsory brand formula and trademark licensing to allow new firms to effectively compete.

Trial of this case was delayed but ultimately it was dismissed by a judge in 1981 finding that the FTC had failed to prove that the firms earned anticompetitive high profits from implicitly coordinating their activities. This dismissal was confirmed by the Commission in 1982 after the FTC had come under Republican leadership (McClure, 1996, 20). This pattern of starting a case in the 1970s only to see it abandoned in the 1980s is common to other FTC anti-brand marketing initiatives.

In 1976, the FTC issued a complaint against General Foods for introducing a temporary "fighting brand" as well as price signaling a proposed market division, and predatory pricing in an attempt to dissuade Folger's from entering the east coast grocery store coffee markets so that Maxwell House could maintain its dominant position. The fighting brand had previously failed in test marketing and was packaged to resemble Folger's package. The judge found the tactics to be anticompetitive, but that Folger's did not have a reasonable probability of success because Folger's was owned by P&G which was larger than General Foods. The Commission affirmed dismissal in 1984, specifically noting in the majority opinion that product differentiation was not an artificial entry barrier in this market but rather distinguished products with different attributes from one another echoing its earlier *Heublein* analysis (*General Foods Corp.*, 1984, 365).

MARKET-DOMINATING TRADEMARKS

The next step for the FTC was to challenge a market-dominating brand arguing that extensive promotion of a trademarked brand name caused consumers to think of the trademarked name as the product category name—i.e., the trademark had become generic.

The Lanham Act allowed it to petition the trademark office to cancel a trademark for just cause such as abandonment, fraud, or genericness. The FTC exercised this authority with mixed success in five cases of abandonment or fraud involving obscure brands between 1950 and 1961 (Shipley, 1978, 13). In 1978, the FTC petitioned its first (and only) "genericness" cancellation request for Formica® before the Trademark Trial and Appeal Board. This also was the FTC's first cancellation request for a well-known trademark (Fietkiewicz, 1980, 439). Cancellation would reduce barriers to competition arising from brand loyalty by allowing other plastic laminate rivals to call their products formica. Consumers would understand that there were many sources of "formica."

During Congressional hearings regarding the FTC's petition, an FTC official enumerated four questions the FTC would examine when considering whether to petition to have a trademark declared generic. First, is there a well-understood generic product name other than the trademark? If so, competitors may use the generic product name and the FTC should not seek to have the trademark declared generic. Second, are consumers unable to readily evaluate the performance and characteristics of the allegedly generic brand and competing brands? Third, does the allegedly generic brand command a price premium and fourth, does the brand dominate the market? If consumers can determine there are equivalent products in the product category, they are less likely to pay a price premium and allowing the trademark to continue does not create an information barrier nor serve as a barrier to market entry (Fietkiewicz, 1980, 466). Eventually, this petition was terminated because Congress refused to fund it.

CASE STUDY: BORDEN–BRAND MARKETING LEGAL CHAMPION

In 1856 Gail Borden Jr. applied for a patent on his method of producing condensed milk that could be stored for long periods of time. The next year he founded his company that later would be known as the Borden Company to honor the company founder. In the 1920s, the Borden Company acquired more than 200 companies to become the largest distributor of liquid milk. It added cheese to its product line and acquired two of the largest ice cream manufacturers in the U.S. (Borden Dairy, 2024).

Meanwhile, in 1911, a Charles E. Borden (no relation to Gail) was recruited with a single share to become a shareholder in the newly formed Borden Ice Cream Company. Shortly afterward, the original Borden sued the new ice cream company seeking an injunction banning the latter from using the name Borden. On appeal, the injunction was denied. The court held that Borden was a personal name and couldn't be granted exclusively to one firm and that original Borden company did not sell ice cream and therefore had lost no business. The court held that an injunction could not be granted based solely on fraud on purchasers as to the identity of the company selling the ice cream (*Borden Ice Cream Co. v. Borden's Condensed Milk Co.*, 1912).

Five years later the Borden Company again lost a similar lawsuit against a company using "Eagle" as a trademark on ice cream cones. "Eagle" was a Borden trademark on its dairy products but not ice cream. The court held that consumer confusion was unlikely because baked cones are a different product from dairy products (*Borden's Condensed Milk Co v. Eagle Manufacturing Co.*, 1917). The reasoning of these two courts was questioned by another court in a 1917 ruling that found trademark infringement of Aunt Jamima pancake mix by Aunt Jemima syrup because consumers would be confused by their similarities into thinking these products were from the same company (*Aunt Jemima Co. v. Rigney & Co.*, 1917). Decades later this became the prevailing view (Fig. 11.1).

Despite these legal setbacks, Borden continued to acquire companies and appear in legal disputes when necessary. First it defended against an

Fig. 11.1 Aunt Jemima Pancake Mix and Syrup Packaging from https://prologue.blogs.archives.gov/2011/08/03/aunt-jemima-what-took-you-so-long/

FTC complaint that it had illegally committed price discrimination by selling private label milk at a lower price than Borden brand milk—a practice it started in 1938. Price discrimination can only be illegal if it occurs between products of the same grade and quality and is likely to cause competitive injury. All the milk produced by Borden was chemically identical.

Upon appeal, the Supreme Court held that "economic factors inherent in brand names and national advertising should not be considered in the jurisdictional inquiry under the statutory 'like grade and quality' test" but rather should be considered under the competitive injury analysis. The Court remanded the case back to the court of appeals for competitive injury analysis and the court found the FTC had not proven likely competitive injury (*FTC v. Borden Co.*, 1966, 383 U.S. 637, 645, 646).

> [T]he price difference creates no competitive advantage to the recipient of the cheaper private brand product on which injury could be predicated. "[R]ather it represents merely a rough equivalent of the benefit by way of the seller's national advertising and promotion which the purchaser of the more expensive branded product enjoys."

With these rulings, Borden helped establish the legitimacy of brand producers also selling product to private labels.

Borden recognized this value of advertising and brand promotion when it acquired ReaLemon-Puritan, producers of the market-dominating ReaLemon brand of reconstituted lemon juice in 1962. Borden paid $12.4 million for net assets with a book value of $2.8 million. This suggests that Borden paid $9.6 million for intangible assets such as the ReaLemon brand (Schmalensee, 1979).

Borden's second legal challenge arose from its acquisition and stimulation of the ReaLemon brand of reconstituted lemon juice. This brand was started in 1935 by Irvin Swartzberg. He began using the "ReaLemon" trademark in the mid-1940s. Sales of the brand grew rapidly and by the 1960s, when it was acquired by Borden, it held about a 90% market share of the reconstituted lemon juice market but only 10% of the lemons and lemon juice market.

In 1974, the FTC filed an administrative complaint challenging Borden's use of selective price cuts to keep regional brands from challenging ReaLemon's dominant market share for processed lemon juice. Two years later, an FTC administrative judge found that the FTC staff had proven the allegations of the complaint and that the source of Borden's monopoly power came from the ReaLemon brand and trademark. The judge also found that investing in brand promotion to differentiate this brand from other physically identical products was an exclusionary anti-competitive tactic (Crane, 2015, 133). Ultimately, the Sixth Circuit Court of Appeals agreed:

> When a seller possesses an overwhelming dominant share of the market … and differentiates its product from others through a recognized and extensively advertised brand name, thereby enabling the seller to control prices or unreasonably restrict competition, then monopoly power may be found to exist. (*Borden Inc. v. FTC*, 1982, 511–512)

The appellate court agreed with the FTC judge that proper relief would include prohibiting sales at unreasonably low prices and Borden licensing the ReaLemon trademark (at one-half of one percent of net sales) to any competitor who wished to use it for a ten-year period. Compulsory licensing would eliminate the barrier to entry created by the brand (Ball, 1978, 486–488; Holmes, 1980, 66–67).

Fortunately for brand marketers who aspire to similar success, the FTC, now with a Republican majority persuaded the Supreme Court to vacate the FTC's original decision and then negotiated a settlement favorable to Borden. Upon accepting the settlement in 1983, the FTC majority acknowledged that brand differentiation served important competitive functions in stimulating inter-brand competition and stated that it could no longer support the condemnation of successful dominant brands in its original opinion (McClure, 1996, 19). It also noted that ironically had the FTC ordered licensing of the ReaLemon trademark to competitors likely would have caused consumer deception regarding which products were the genuine brand and which were imitations—possibly of lower quality. As discussed above, some of the earliest FTC cases involved preventing this sort of "passing off."

Some criticized the ReaLemon litigation and the Formica proceeding as a two-pronged attack against trademarks (Fietkiewicz, 1980, 465–468). Both alleged the brand name operated in the minds of consumers as a generic product name (Shipley, 1978, 27). However, in its proceeding against Borden, the FTC was challenging various tactics that Borden allegedly used to maintain its monopoly position, not the "genericness" of the name itself as in the Formica proceeding.

REFERENCES

Bain, J. S. (1956). *Barriers to New Competition*. Harvard University Press.

Ball, W. H. (1978). Government Versus Trademarks: Today—Pharmaceuticals, Realemon and Formica—Tomorrow? *The Trademark Reporter, 68*(4), 471–504.

Barnes, S. N., & Oppenheim, S. C. (1955). *The Attorney General's National Committee to Study the Antitrust Laws*. Government Printing Office.

Borden Co. v. FTC. (1967). 381 F. 2d 175 (5th Cir.).

Borden's Condensed Milk Co v. Eagle Manufacturing Co. (1917). 47 App. D.C. 191 (D.C.C.A).

Borden Dairy. (2024). *History*. https://www.bordendairy.com/press-room/history/

Borden Ice Cream Co. v. Borden's Condensed Milk Co., (1912), 201 F. 510 (7th Cir.).

Borden, Inc. v. FTC (1982). 674 F.2d 498 (6th Cir.), *vacated*, 461 U.S. 940 (1983).

Brown, R. S., Jr. (1948). Advertising and the Public Interest: Legal Protection of Trade Symbols. *Yale Law Journal, 57*(7), 1165–1206.

Brown, W. F. (1947). The Federal Trade Commission and False Advertising II. *Journal of Marketing, 12*(2), 193–201.

Chase, S., & Schlink, F. J. (1927). *Your Money's Worth: A Study in the Waste of the Consumer's Dollar*. The Macmillan Co.

Chen, C. (1992). Food and Drug Administration Food Standards of Identity: Consumer Protection Through the Regulation of Product Information. *Food and Drug Law Journal, 47*(2), 185–206.

Comanor, W. S., & Wilson, T. A. (1967). Advertising, Market Structure and Performance. *The Review of Economics and Statistics, 49*(4), 423–440.

Comanor, W. S., & Wilson, T. A. (1974). *Advertising and Market Power*. Harvard University Press.

Crane, D. A. (2015). Brands and Market Power: A Bird's Eye View. In D. R. Desai, J. Lianos, & S. W. Waller (Eds.), *Brands, Competition Law and IP* (pp. 128–137). Cambridge University.

Federal Trade Commission. (1981). *Staff Task Force Report on Comparative Performance Information*. Government Printing Office.

Fietkiewicz, J. M. (1980). Section 14 of the Lanham Act–FTC Authority to Challenge Generic Trademarks. *Fordham Law Review, 48*(4), 437–470.

Food and Drug Administration. (2018). *Food Standard Innovations: Peanut Butter's Sticky Standard*. https://www.fda.gov/about-fda/histories-product-regulation/food-standard-innovations-peanut-butters-sticky-standard

FTC v. Borden Co. (1966). 383 US 637 (Supreme Court).

FTC v. Proctor & Gamble Co. (1967), 386 U.S. 568 (Supreme Court).

Galbraith, J. K. (1958). *The Affluent Society*. Houghton Mifflin Harcourt.

General Foods Corp. v. FTC (1967), 386 F.2d 936 (3rd Cir.), *cert. denied,* 391 U.S. 919 (1968).

General Foods Corp. (1984), 103 F.T.C. 204.

Holmes, W. C. (1980). Compulsory Patent and Trademark Licensing: A Framework for Analysis. *Loyola University Law Journal, 12*(1), 43–77.

Heublein, Inc. (1980). 96 F.T.C. 385.

Kaldor, N. V. (1950, February). The Economic Aspects of Advertising. *Review of Economic Studies, 18,* 1–27.

McClure, D. M. (1996). Trademarks and Competition: The Recent History. *Law and Contemporary Problems, 59*(Spring), 13–43.

Merrill, R. A., & Collier, E. M. (1974, May). 'Like Mother Used to Make': An Analysis of FDA Food Standards of Identity. *Columbia Law Review, 74,* 561–614.

Packard, V. (1958). *The Hidden Persuaders.* Pocket Books.

Pattishall, B. W. (1952). Trade-Marks and the Monopoly Phobia. *Michigan Law Review, 50*(7), 967–990.

Petty, R. D. (2016). U.S. Antitrust Law and the Practice of Marketing. In D. G. B. Jones & M. Tadajewski (Eds.), *The Routledge Companion to Marketing History* (pp. 255–276). Routledge.

Petty, R. D. (2018). The US Battle Against Brand Marketing: Circa 1930–1980. *Journal of Historical Research in Marketing, 10*(1), 60–85.

Richards, J. I., & Petty, R. D. (2007). Advertising Regulation. In G. J. Tellis & T. Ambler (Eds.), *The Sage Handbook of Advertising* (pp. 383–397). Sage Publications.

Schmalensee, R. (1979). On the Use of Economic Models In Antitrust: The Realemon Case. *University of Pennsylvania Law Review, 127*(4), 994. https://scholarship.law.upenn.edu/penn_law_review/vol127/iss4/18

Shipley, D. E. (1978). Generic Trademarks, the FTC and the Lanham Act: Covering the Market with Formica. *William and Mary Law Review, 20*(1), 1–32.

Stigler, G. J. (1961). The Economics of Information. *Journal of Political Economy, 69*(3), 213–225.

Telser, L. G. (1964). Advertising and Competition. *Journal of Political Economy, 72*(December), 537–562.

Williamson, J. R. (1995). *Federal Antitrust Policy During the Kennedy-Johnson Years.* Greenwood Press.

CHAPTER 12

Conclusion: Have Brand Marketers Gained Too Much Control?

Abstract This chapter concludes the centuries old evolution of small insignificant trade markings to modern brands that seek to attract consumer interest and ultimately loyalty in purchasing. It examines trademark dilution and the interaction between trademarks and domain names. It suggests that some brand marketers seek to use their marks to reduce competition with other branded products to the detriment of consumers. The chapter ends with a case study of 1-800 Contacts which barely defeated antitrust charges against its allegedly abusive conduct.

Keywords 1-800 Contacts · Trademark Dilution · Domain Names · Trademark Trolls · Brand Bullies

History indicates that simple branding or marking products has evolved to promote the brand so that consumers can easily search for it rather than search for various products' details. Furthermore, promoting the brand itself can cause consumers to develop an attachment to the brand image pleasing consumers when they purchase or use the brand. Brand marketers have pushed for increasing protection under trademark law including registration and the ability to challenge applications for registration. In addition, infringement has extended beyond names and logos to

© The Author(s), under exclusive license to Springer Nature Switzerland AG 2024
R. D. Petty, *From Marking Products to Marketing Brands*, Palgrave Studies in Marketing, Organizations and Society,
https://doi.org/10.1007/978-3-031-76778-4_12

cover other brand identifiers and relaxing the requirement that infringement could only occur within the same industry (Carter 1990). Just recently, the Trademark Modernization Act of 2020 provides trademark holders who proven infringement or dilution with a rebuttable presumption of irreparable harm making it easier to obtain an injunction against the imitator.

Since the 1980s when the FTC gave up its anti-brand activities, brand marketing in the U.S. has become so well accepted today that even what appears to recent critiques of brand marketing such as *No Logo: Taking Aim at the Brand Bullies* by Naomi Klein (1999) and *Brand Name Bullies: The Quest to Own and Control Culture* by David Bollier (2005) are commentary not on brand marketing per se but rather are an expose' of activism against global corporations and criticisms of efforts to extend copyright and trademark law to control cultural expression, respectively. Indeed today, monopoly concerns about either trademark protection of generic terms or antitrust analysis of a single-brand product market are rare (Desai & Waller, 2015, 86–97).

This chapter begins by examining two modern phenomena—trademark dilution and the acquisition and use of internet domain names. It then discusses the potential for trademark abuse. It concludes with a case study of a firm using trademarks in the era of the internet.

DILUTION OF FAMOUS TRADEMARKS

This modern general acceptance of brand marketing enabled by trademark law has allowed an apparent paradigm shift—Frank Schecter's 1927 proposal regarding trademark dilution protection for famous trademarks was finally enacted federally in 1995. Dilution cases represent a fundamental shift in trademark law because they don't require proving consumer confusion about product source or that the two marks be used in the same or similar industries. Even though consumers might not be confused about brand identities (the source of the trademarked product), dilution still allows brand marketers to challenge unauthorized uses of their famous trademarks, even in completely different industries. Dilution of trademarks across unrelated industries is consistent with marketing scholarship advocating that existing brand names could profitably be extended into new product categories (Ries & Trout, 1981; Tauber, 1981). This started the brand marketing literature that exploded in the 1990s (Petty, 2011, 86).

Dilution is only applicable to famous marks. Fame is proven by evidence that when the general public encounters the mark it associates the term with the mark owner. Dilution of a trademark may occur by blurring or tarnishment. The former arises from similarity between marks that diminishes the famous mark's distinctiveness while the latter is caused by associations that harm the reputation of the famous mark. While similarities of the products are not considered under dilution, similarity of the marks is considered, and courts have recently clarified they don't necessarily have to be identical or nearly identical (*Levi Strauss & Co. v. Abercrombie & Fitch Trading Co.*, 2011).

A study of dilution court decisions found that during the early years after the statute was enacted, about half the cases ordered relief for dilution (most dilution cases also claimed infringement). This dropped to less than 25% by 2003 (Long, 2006, 1042). Eleven years after its enactment, the statute was revised to clarify that plaintiffs only need to prove a likelihood of dilution rather than actual dilution. Presumably, this should increase the proportion of cases that win dilution relief. Dilution is poised to become a substantial expansion of trademark rights for brand marketers. While brand marketers will benefit from this expansion, whether it benefits consumers is subject to discussion.

Domain Names

Today, shopping for branded goods and services using the internet is commonplace to say the least. Farley (2023) suggests that technology such as Artificial Intelligence could make online product searches so easy that the reduction-of-search-costs rationale for trademarks may no longer be valid at least in the online context. A new rationale may need to be developed for the future that includes trademark law as well as domain name rules since brand marketers typically seek domain names and social media hashtags that are similar to their trademarks or common product category names which cannot be trademarked. Domain names, including those for product categories, are available to the first applicant or the highest bidder if an auction is held. For example, "insure.com" sold for $16 million and "hotels.com" for $11 million. Many firms have multiple websites addresses to improve marketing coverage.

Whereas trademarks are registered in industry categories and only exclusive within those categories, domain names once granted are exclusive over the entire internet. Furthermore, while trademark registrars will consider whether a proposed mark is too similar to an existing mark, the Internet Corporation for Assigned Names and Numbers (ICANN) will allow domain names that are only one digit different than an existing domain name. The differences between trademarks and domain names are summarized in Table 12.1.

Until recently, top-level domain names have been limited to twenty-two specific words such as "-.net," "-.biz" and "-.com," with the latter being far and away the most popular choice. Because of a perceived shortage of "-.com" addresses, ICANN decided to expand the number of available domain names through its new generic top-level domain name (gTLD) program. Under this new program, applicants may seek to operate a domain name registry for an address ending in virtually any word or set of letters including brand names like "-.ford" or generic/descriptive words such as "-.car." These new options may be particularly attractive to firms that do not currently control their "brand.com" or "categorylabel.com" domain name. Some estimate that only about 600 of the original applications for the new program were for trademarked brand names and nearly 1300 for generic categories such as "-.book," "-.store" and "-.app." The latter was the most contested name with thirteen applicants (Petty, 2015).

Non-generic or descriptive domain names also may receive trademark law protection if they are distinctive and function to identify the source of products (brand) for consumers. The same is true for hashtags like "#McDstories." Court decisions have consistently held that the mere registration of a trademarked word or phrase as a domain name does not constitute use of the mark in commerce as required for trademark protection. Particularly, if the new website is "in progress." Marketers must present evidence that the domain name is actually used by consumers as a source identifier and therefore merits protection as a trademark. Generic or purely descriptive domain names such as "patents.com" will not be protected as trademarks. The addition of a top-level domain name such as "-.com" does not affect trademark analysis in determining whether a word is generic or pure descriptive (Petty, 2016).

A specific U.S. statute condemns cybersquatting, the bad faith registration or selling of a domain name that is identical or confusingly similar to a registered trademark or dilutive of a famous trademark (15 U.S.C. §§ 1125(d) and 1129). The statute specifically includes typosquatting—the intentional misspelling of a trademarked in a domain name mentioned above. The misspelled word is almost always confusingly similar to the

Table 12.1 Domain names compared to trademarks from Petty (2016, 136)

Issue	Domain Names (DNs)	Trademarks (TMs)
Similarity	DNs do not conflict if they are not identical. However, cybersquatting covers DNs that are either identical or similar to TMs	TMs conflict if they are confusingly similar to each other in meaning, sound or appearance (including typeface, color, logo design, etc.) or likely to dilute a famous mark
Descriptiveness	DNs may be generically descriptive such as drugstore.com	TMs may not be generic and may only be descriptive if secondary meaning is shown. However, a generic term may be used as an arbitrary mark for an unrelated product category such as APPLE computers and APPLE records
Classes of Goods and Services	DNs may only be assigned to one user and therefore cover all goods and services	TMs are registered for specified classes of goods and services, so that the same mark may be registered by different parties in different classes of goods and services. There may still be an issue of infringement if the classes are sufficiently close to confuse consumers or cause dilution
Geographic Scope	DNs are registered once for a period of time and are good throughout the world. They may be renewed	TMs must be protected on a country-by-country basis. The TRIPS agreement requires protection of famous, but unregistered marks and the Madrid Protocol allows for a single application to be used for multiple countries

trademark. It also would cover combosquatting—the addition of other words to a trademark as a domain name, e.g., "buytoyota.net." The statute lists nine non-exclusive factors that courts may consider when determining whether there is "bad faith intent to profit." Essentially the factors boil down to whether the registrant has a legitimate interest in the domain named as evidenced by prior use or perhaps non-commercial use versus evidence of bad faith such as false contact information, offer to transfer the domain name to the owner of a closely similar or identical trademark, intent to divert customers from the trademark owner's website, or the registration of multiple similar names (Petty, 2016).

By awarding such generic registries to marketers of the product, ICANN may be doing what trademark law has attempted to prevent for over a century—granting a single firm exclusive rights to a generic product category creating the historically feared "trademark monopoly" would make it more difficult for competitors to promote their products to consumers (Folsom & Teply, 1980). Trademark law does allow generic terms to be used in collective and certification trademarks, but such marks must be available to qualified organization members or firms rather than arbitrarily allocated to some but not others. It remains to be seen whether ICAAN will impose similar open availability requirements for generic or merely descriptive domain names.

TRADEMARK MISUSE

Trademarks violations and domain names that are confusingly similar to trademarks are pursued everyday by large firms often against smaller firms. Just because it is a "David vs. Goliath" situation does not mean that brand marketers are abusing their trademarks. In fact, trademark registrants are required to enforce their marks against infringement or dilution or risk a finding the mark has been abandoned. The registrant then would lose its rights over that trademark. For this reason, trademark registrants usually monitor the internet (including domain name registries) and trademark applications for similar marks.

When an imitation is spotted, the original trademark registrant will send a "cease and desist" letter to the party responsible for the imitation. In many cases, the letter is well thought out and offers a compelling explanation why the letter recipient should stop what it's doing. However, in other cases, firms send out letters based on a cursory finding of similarity. While sometimes such cursory analysis might still find legitimate imitation concerns, in other cases, the letter writer may be embarrassed by sending a letter to a child or grandparent. Letters also may be written in intimidating "legalese" and signed by a lawyer. They typically threaten expensive litigation with expensive appeals if needed (Grinvald, 2011, 643–650). A study of reported trademark court cases found that 5.5% of these cases were trademark bullying because the court issued a summary judgment against the defendant. This results in the case being dismissed without a trial because the complaint is inadequate on its face to prove the defendant violated the law. Of course, many cases are settled so 5.5% is the minimum proportion of bullying cases (Port, 2014).

There are at least two types of trademark abusers. The first is the Trademark Troll named for trolls in English and Norse legend who live under bridges and attack anyone who tries to use the bridge seeking payment of a toll or to eat the bridge trespasser depending on which version of the myth you prefer. A Trademark Troll registers a number of trademarks (usually under intent-to-use) and/or domain names and then contacts the legitimate registrants seeking either a periodic fee or outright sale. The latter will require notifying the registration authorities of the change in ownership. This may occur when there are rumors about a merger or new product introduction and the Troll guesses about likely new names that will be used. This also may occur in countries where well-known international brands have not yet entered. A local Troll registers the brand name, in English or local languages, and waits for entry of the international brand to enter the country and negotiate the lease or sale of the local trademark name.

The classic example of a Trademark Troll is Leo Stoller who registered Stealth as a trademark in several industries. He then asserted trademark infringement against anyone using that word, including a movie title. He filed nearly 50 cases in the District Court of Northern Illinois, regarding lost all of them and was ordered to pay costs and attorneys fees of the defendant in at least six cases. When he sued the makers of Stealth baseball bats, the target struck back and the court ordered Stoller to pay the defendant's attorneys' fees and costs and also ordered the Stealth registration be canceled (Folgers, 2007).

Like Trademark Trolls, Brand Bullies, the second form of trademark abusers, also base their cease and desist letters on an unreasonable interpretation of their trademark rights and design their letters to be intimidating and even threatening. The difference between Trademark Trolls and Brand Bullies is that the former seek money from a licensing agreement or an outright sale of imitation mark or domain name, while the latter want the imitator to stop its imitation. A single abuser might pursue close rivals as a Brand Bully while at the same time approach non-rivals as a Trademark Troll. Of course, for a high enough price, a Brand Bully might be persuaded to become a Troll.

Grinvald (2011) defines trademark bullies to require a large firm threatening a smaller one. J. Shechtman (2023) wants a pattern of behavior to help define trademark misuse. However, there are lots of examples like Leo Stoller where a small firm attacks larger firms as a nuisance hoping for a quick settlements. In addition, there are plenty of examples where a legitimate brand owner sues the creator of a brand parody and might not use such lawsuits as a typical business practice. Brand Bullies are likely to pursue brand parodies particularly if they might tarnish the targeted brand. They might also pursue store brand products alleging they are too similar to their well-known branded product and its packaging (Petty, 2016, 343–348).

In any event, the goal of trademark abusive behavior is to limit competition and raise revenue by imposing licensing fees on other firms. Ultimately consumers bear the burden of such practices from price increases to cover higher costs and less optimal search for desirable brands become some useful names are not available in some industries. Time will tell if dilution or domain names will add or subtract from these problems (Fig. 12.1).

Case Study: 1-800 Contacts Lawsuits

This case study involves a firm, 1-800 Contacts, who arguably behaved like a Brand Bully attacking rivals to get them to stop buying and using the 1-800 Contacts trademarked name as a keyword trigger search screen pop-up advertising. Over time, it successfully negotiated settlements with thirteen other contact lens retailers where both sides agreed not to use the other's trademarks as advertising keywords. The Federal Trade Commission (FTC) then sued arguing this was a market division conspiracy that violated the antitrust laws.

1-800 Contacts is the oldest prescription-by-mail optical company that's still operating today and is currently the largest contact lens retailer in the United States. It started as a mail-order contact lens business in a college dorm in 1992 and its current name was adopted in 1995 when it obtained the 1-800 Contacts telephone number. Once the company

Fig. 12.1 Trademark misuse

began advertising the 1-800 Contacts name and phone number, it saw a 20% to 25% increase in customer acquisition and customer retention. The following year, the company launched its website and by 2004, its internet sales exceeded its telephone sales. In 2015, 1-800 Contacts' revenues were approximately $460 million.

1-800 Contacts' first pop-up advertising lawsuit occurred when it sued WhenU and Vision Direct. WhenU supplied pop-up advertising during consumer internet searches based on keywords. When Vision Direct (and others) purchased "1-800 Contacts" as a keyword, a Vision Direct ad would pop-up when consumers arrived at the search engine results page or the 1-800 Contacts website. 1-800 Contacts argued this was inherently deceptive because consumers would believe the pop-up ad came from the underlying webpage rather than an outside party. Although initially successful in obtaining a preliminary injunction, the appellate court declared the practice was legal under trademark law, because consumers never saw the keywords, so this practice did not constitute trademark use in commerce (*1-800 Contacts, Inc. v. WhenU.com*, 2005). This decision was followed eight years later when the Tenth Circuit Court of Appeals also held that another competitor, Lens.com, did not commit trademark infringement when it purchased search advertisements using 1-800 Contacts' federally registered 1800 CONTACTS trademark as a keyword (*1-800 Contacts, Inc. v. Lens.com, Inc.*, 2013).

Meanwhile, the FTC started an investigation of 1-800 Contacts' litigation and settlement practices regarding advertising keywords. It found that 1-800 Contacts sent out numerous cease and desist orders between 2005 and 2010 alleging the keyword practice was illegal—contrary to Second Circuit WhenU opinion. 1-800 Contacts then settled with the following firms, each agreeing not to purchase keywords containing competitors' trademarks and to employ negative keywords so that a search including one party's trademarks will not trigger a display of the other party's ads.: AC Lens (Feb. 18, 2010), Contact Lens King (Mar. 8, 2010), Empire Vision (Feb. 25, 2010), EZ Contacts USA (Dec. 6, 2007), Lensfast (Dec. 23, 2008), Lenses for Less (Jan. 20, 2010), Lens.com (Aug. 13, 2007), LensWorld (Jan. 8, 2008), Memorial Eye (Dec. 23, 2008), Standard Optical (July 13, 2010), Tram Data (May 6, 2010), Walgreens (June 8, 2010), and Web Eye Care (Aug. 10, 2010) (*in re 1-800-Contacts, Inc.*, 2018).

The FTC concluded that the agreements violated antitrust law, hurting consumers by blocking ads that would inform them that identical products were available at lower prices and reducing competition for keywords. Due to the alleged agreements, the plaintiffs and other consumers were reportedly denied the ability to search online advertisements for the best deals when looking for contacts. As a result, they allegedly paid higher prices for contact lenses. In reversing the FTC's decision, a Federal court of appeals concluded that keyword bidding agreements in this case offered pro-competitive justifications including protecting trademarks and preventing confusion in the marketplace.

Based on the FTC decision, before the appeal was decided, 1-800 Contacts and several other firms agreed to settle a private consumer class action lawsuit for $40 million. 1-800 Contacts promised to contribute $15.2 million, Walgreens and Vision Direct will contribute $12 million, AC Lens and National Vision will contribute $7 million, and Luxottica will contribute $5.9 million. The defendants in this 2020 settlement did not admit any wrongdoing but they did pay expenses to contest the FTC cases and pay some reparations to consumers.

REFERENCES

1-800 Contacts Class Action Settlement. (2020). https://topclassactions.com/ lawsuit-settlements/closed-settlements/1-800-contacts-class-action-settle

ment/#:~:text=Several%20contacts%20providers%20including%201,%3A%
201%2D800%20from%20Jan

1-800 Contacts, Inc. v. Lens.com, Inc. (2013), 722 F.3d 1229 (10th Cir.).

1-800 Contacts, Inc. v. Federal Trade Commission. (2021). 1 F.4th 192 (2d Cir.).

1-800 Contacts, Inc. v. WhenU.com. (2005). 414 F.3d 400 (2d Cir.).

in re 1-800-Contacts, Inc. (2018). Opinion of the Federal Trade Commission.

Bollier, D. (2005). *Brand Name Bullies: The Quest to Own and Control Culture.* Wiley.

Carter, S. L. (1990). The Trouble with Trademark. *The Yale Law Journal, 99*(4), 759–800.

Desai, D. R., & Waller, S. W. (2015). Brands, Competition, and Antitrust Law. In D. R. Desai, I. Lianos, & S. W. Waller (Eds.), *Brands, Competition Law and IP* (pp. 75–112). Cambridge University.

Farley, C. H. (2023). Trademarks in an Algorithmic World. *Washington Law Review, 98*(4), 1123–1185. Available at SSRN: https://ssrn.com/abstract=4699501

Folgers, A. B. (2007). The Seventh Circuit's Approach to Deterring the Trademark Troll: Say Goodbye to Your Registration and Pay the Costs of Litigation. *Seventh Circuit Review, 3*(1), 452–490.

Folsom, R. H., & Teply, L. L. (1980). Trademarked Generic Words. *The Yale Law Journal, 89*(7), 1323–1359.

Grinvald, L. C. (2011). Shaming Trademark Bullies. *Wisconsin Law Review, 2011*(3), 625–689.

Klein, N. (1999). *No Logo: Taking Aim at the Brand Bullies.* Picador.

Lemley, M. A., Goldman, E. (2019, September 12). *Amicus Brief of 29 IP, Internet Law, & Antitrust Professors in 1-800 Contacts v. F.T.C* (Stanford Law and Economics Olin Working Paper No. 538). Available at SSRN: https://ssrn.com/abstract=3452884 or https://doi.org/10.2139/ssrn.3452884

Levi Strauss & Co. v. Abercrombie & Fitch Trading Co. (2011), 633 F.3d 1158 (9th Cir.).

Long, C. (2006). Dilution. *Columbia Law Review, 106*(5), 1029–1078. https://scholarship.law.columbia.edu/faculty_scholarship/128

Petty R. D. (2011). The Co-development of Trademark Law and the Concept of Brand Marketing in the U.S. before 1946. *Journal of Macromarketing, 31*(1), 85–99.

Petty, R. D. (2015). After the Dot: Marketing Policy Issues with the New Generic Top Level Domain Names Program. In S. M. Baker & M. Mason (Eds.), *2015 Marketing and Public Policy Conference Proceedings* (pp. 38–42).

Petty, R. D. (2016). *Branding Law: Guide to the Legal Issues in Brand Management.* West Academic.

Port, K. L. (2014). Trademark Extortion Revisited: A Response to Vogel and Schacter. *Chicago-Kent Journal of Intellectual Property, 14*(Fall), 217–232.

Ries, A., & Trout, J. (1981). *Positioning: The Battle for Your Mind*. McGraw Hill.

Shechtman, J. (2023, December). No Bullying Allowed Here: Adopting a Misuse Doctrine to Defeat Trademark Bullies. *Cardozo Law Review, 45*, 686–719.

Tauber, E. M. (1981). Brand Franchise Extension: New Product Benefits from Existing Brand Names. *Business Horizons, 24*(2), 36–41.

INDEX

.

The manufacturer's authorised representative in the EU is Springer
Nature Customer Service Centre GmbH, Europaplatz 3, 69115 Heidelberg,
Germany. If you have any concerns regarding our products, please
contact ProductSafety@springernature.com

Printed and bound by CPI Group (UK) Ltd, Croydon, CR0 4YY

27/04/2026

02097604-0002